RONA MUNRO

Rona Munro has written for stage, radio, television and film since 1982. Her recent stage credits include *Bold Girls* for 7:84 Scotland and subsequently Hampstead Theatre (Evening Standard Most Promising Playwright Award 1991) and *Your Turn to Clean the Stair* for the Traverse Theatre, Edinburgh, (1992).

Her television play *Men of the Month*, directed by Jean Stewart, was shown on BBC 2 in 1994, and her first feature film *Ladybird, Ladybird*, directed by Ken Loach was also released that year.

Rona was born and brought up in North East Scotland and writes for the Aberdonian feminist comedy act *The Misfits*.

By the same author

YOUR TURN TO CLEAN THE STAIR (includes FUGUE)
BOLD GIRLS in FIRST RUN 3, edited by Matthew Lloyd

A selection of other titles from Nick Hern Books

Caryl Churchill
CHURCHILL: SHORTS
CLOUD NINE
ICECREAM
LIGHT SHINING IN
    BUCKINGHAMSHIRE
MAD FOREST
THE SKRIKER
TRAPS

John Clifford
INES DE CASTRO (in FIRST
    RUN 2, ed.Kate Harwood)
THE LIGHT IN THE
    VILLAGE

Helen Edmundson
ANNA KARENINA
THE CLEARING
THE MILL ON THE FLOSS

Chris Hannan
THE EVIL DOERS
    & THE BABY

Clare McIntyre
MY HEART'S A SUITCASE
    & LOW LEVEL PANIC

Kim Morrissey
DORA

Phyllis Nagy
BUTTERFLY KISS
THE STRIP

Ludmila Petrushevskaya
CINZANO - Eleven Plays

Seneca
(trans Caryl Churchill)
THYESTES

Claire Tomalin
THE WINTER WIFE

Sophie Treadwell
MACHINAL

Michel Tremblay
THE GUID SISTERS

SCOT-FREE New Scottish Plays
    ed. Alasdair Cameron

John Byrne WRITER'S CRAMP

John Clifford LOSING VENICE

Anne Marie Di Mambro
    THE LETTER-BOX

Chris Hannan ELIZABETH
    GORDON QUINN

John McKay DEAD DAD DOG

Rona Munro SATURDAY AT
    THE COMMODORE

Tony Roper THE STEAMIE

RONA MUNRO

THE MAIDEN STONE

NICK HERN BOOKS
London

A **Nick Hern Book**

The Maiden Stone first published in Great Britain in 1995
as a paperback original by Nick Hern Books, 14 Larden Road,
London W3 7ST

The Maiden Stone copyright © 1995 by Rona Munro

Rona Munro has asserted her right to be identified as
author of this Work

Front cover: from design by Sears Davies Ltd

Typeset by Country Setting, Woodchurch, Kent TN26 3TB
Printed by Athenaeum Press Ltd, Gateshead, Tyne & Wear

A CIP catalogue record for this book is available
from the British Library

ISBN 1 85459 243 2

100064798

Author's Note

The Maiden Stone was commissioned by Hampstead Theatre.
It's a play about my own birthplace, North East Scotland. That
landscape remains for me one of the most beautiful I know
though its effect on me, like its own mountains, is deceptive.
It's only when you reach the summit and look back you realise
the distance you've come and see you're standing on top of the
world.

The language of the piece is the native dialect as I remember it
and is in no sense historical but a living language. For the
Hampstead production we reproduced this with minimal
compromise and I don't think the rhythm or the integrity of the
play would survive any attempt at translation. The dialect is not
rigidly consistent but this reflects the true rhythms of bilingual
speech, i.e. not *every* 'have' becomes 'hae'.

It is important for the story of the play to be told as described
but I would anticipate staging which is stylised enough to allow
the suggestion of hordes of children, trees, fire and snow without these necessarily being literally present. In particular I see
the 'brood' functioning as a kind of chorus and mechanism to
create some of the events of the piece and not as an actual
horde of toddlers.

There was at least one nineteenth-century actress who has left
us a record of her wanderings. She toured as far north as
Arbroath, had seventeen children and outlived two husbands.

The landscape is real as is the Maiden Stone. Corgarff Castle is
real and well haunted by the ghosts of lonely red coats. Auchnibeck is invented but typical of a N.E. 'toun' of the period.
The songs and stories are ones I remember from childhood.
I suppose I feel them to be a record of a people and a culture
invisible in history but a bedrock I stand on nonetheless.

I have taken some small liberties with time, distance and
language but I think, like Bidie, you can change the tale if it
makes for a better story, everything larger than detail is as real
as I can make it.

For Joelle, for all the roads and Saff,
for all the homecomings

Characters

HARRIET – Early forties but looking good on it despite her situation. She is from the North of England but retains no trace of this in her voice except in moments of stress.

BIDIE – Late thirties but appears older than HARRIET. She is a travelling woman.

MARY – Sixteen. Her clothes suggest something better than a farm worker, their condition suggests something worse.

MIRIAM – Fourteen. Harriet's daughter.

ARCHIE – Thirty-five. Scottish but not a North Easter.

NICK – Could be anything from thirty-five to fifty-five. A traveller.

CHILDREN – HARRY, babies and BIDIE's brood.

The Maiden Stone was first performed at the Hampstead
Theatre, London on 21 April 1995. Press night: 27 April.
The cast was as follows:

HARRIET	Frances Tomelty
BIDIE	Carol Ann Crawford
MARY	Shirley Henderson
MIRIAM	Sarah Howe
ARCHIE	Paul Higgins
NICK	Alexander Morton
HARRY	Anthony Colbert

Bidie's Brood
Team A: Christopher Frost, Lydia Hrela, Perry Keating,
Natalie King, Katie Sheehy

Team B: Bradley Cassidy, Mae Cassidy, Gemma Coughlan,
Owen Proktor-Jackson, Samantha Wadsworth

Directed by Matthew Lloyd
Set Designer Robin Don
Costume Designer Anne Sinclair
Lighting Designer Robert Bryan
Choreographer Rosemary Lee
Composer Jim Sutherland
Sound Designer Simon Whitehorn
Dialect Coach Julia Wilson-Dickson
Hair and Make-up Consultant Louise Fisher

Once upon a time . . .
In a place like Donside . . .

ACT ONE

*Farm and woodland in North East Scotland. The hills are
visible in the distance over a sweep of fields. There is a dry
stone dyke on stage . One larger stone, an earlier monolith, the
Maiden Stone had been embedded in the dyke. It resembles a
crude human figure, leaning forward as if running.*

There is a road, unmetalled, a farm track between stone dykes.

It is late summer.

Scene One

The road. Dusk.

BIDIE *walks to centre stage. She has a baby on her hip, she's
singing to it softly.*

BIDIE. And wi' you, and wi' you,
　　And wi' you Johnnie lad,
　　I'll dance the buckles aff my shoon
　　Wi' you my Johnnie lad

　　O, Johnnie's nae a gentleman,
　　Nor yet is he a laird,
　　But I would follow Johnnie lad,
　　Although he was a caird.

　　And wi' you, and wi' you,
　　And wi' you Johnnie lad,
　　I'll dance the buckles aff my shoon
　　Wi' you my Johnnie lad.

*While she has been singing a crowd of children have crept
in. They flow around her, stroking her face, combing her
hair. She kisses and pats them as she sings and talks. They
kneel and stand around her, one kneels on all fours to make
a seat, two on either side make arm rests, they have lambs
and dogs and other animals,* BIDIE *sits on a throne of
children and beasts.*

Johnnie was sleeping in the green wood. A giant cam.
Bending doon the tree tops tae see fit he fancies tae chew
on. He spied Johnnie. He caught him up and carried him
home oer his back. He says tae Johnnie, 'Go get me twa
eggs frae the siller hawk tae hae til my dinner or I'll eat you
now and pick my teeth wi' your shin bane.' Johnnie grat. It
wis the ogre's belly for him. But the giant's dochter cam tae
him. She'd pity for him. She wiped his face wi' her reid hair
and took him intae the forest.

They could see the siller hawk, riding the sough o' a cauld
blue wind, a wee white ash flake at the roof o' the forest.
Her nest wis as high as the clouds, up a pine tree wi' a trunk
as slippery as copper and nae branches tae it at a'.

The giant's dochter pu's aff a' her fingers and sticks them
on the tree and that wis his ladder tae the nest. Her ain
bleeding fingers.

Next day, he wis set tae clean a giant byre full o' sharn fae a
hundred years o' giant beasts. The giant's dochter took aff
her goon and dammed the stream wi' her body tae drive the
burn through the byre and wash it clean. Next day he wis tae
catch a' the birds that flew. She made a net o' her hair and
caught them for him. Then they lay together. Then she freed
him oot that dungeon and he took her hame.

He left her at the castle gate and went in tae get her a goon.
Once through his ain gate he forgot her altogether.

He was awa tae get merriet, riding doon the street wi' his
feeance, a wee blonde girl jist oot the egg. A craw and a
hawk and a cooshie doo ca'd his name and he turned and
saw her at the gate. Her hair's aff, her hand bleedin and
she's naked yet. He fell aff his horse and ran tae kiss her.
They say . . . They say they got merriet . . .

BIDIE *laughs again, raises the baby and kisses it.*

I say she held his bairn up tae him. She let him see his eyes
in its face. Then she took it awa wi' her intae the forest,
Johnnie's eyes an a'. Is that nae foo it should finish?

The children swirl round her again they dance off together.

And god help the wee blonde lassie wi' eggshell still in her
hair. (*Singing.*) An wi' you, an' wi' you , an wi' you Johnnie

lad, I'll dance the buckles aff my shoon wi' you my bonny lad . . .

Scene Two

The farm, mid afternoon.

Lights up on HARRIET.

HARRIET *is walking to and fro in front of a pile of props and bags. Both HARRIET and her luggage have been abandoned at the entrance to a farmyard. She is reading from a half finished letter.*

HARRIET. They do not speak English . . .

HARRIET *peers at her letter a moment then looks at her baggage behind her. She puts the letter down carefully, weighting it with a stone. She takes out a portable writing desk and sets it up on the dyke. Drawing out a pen she makes a tiny addition to her letter. She waves it in the air to dry then notices she has trodden in something. She wipes her foot against the grass then breathing heavily in irritation grabs a sheaf of writing paper and scrubs at her shoe. She continues reading.*

They are a bleak and ignorant people, tied by ignorance to a bleak and salt scarred landscape. I well know, my dear sister, that there will be many who would delight in seeing where the pursuit of love and talent have led me. I trust you will be my defender against such cramped minds and will assure them that I am indeed crossing new frontiers in a career they cannot diminish with their petty judgements. In truth, however, even the landscape has become flat and lost the grandeur of the mountains to the west although we may be grateful that the perils of weather and bandits are also behind us. The North East of this country has something of the aspect of a blasted heath, a poet's vision of an icy purgatory. The people do not make poems from it. They make turnips and cattle feed.

As to my daughters, it is with the emotion only a mother could understand that I read your news of them . . .

Turns sees MARY. MARY *bobs a curtsey.* HARRIET *regards her icily for a minute.* MARY *bobs again.* HARRIET *lowers her letter.*

Yes?

MARY *bobs again.*

MARY. I'm Mary, mistress. Thank you, mistress.

HARRIET. What do you want?

MARY. I'm tae help.

HARRIET *regards her a moment longer, then moves closer looking* MARY *up and down.*

HARRIET (*to herself*). I doubt you'll have enough. (*Speaking slowly with exaggerated clarity.*) It's twins. Did they tell you it was twins?

MARY (*blank*). Na.

HARRIET. You're the wet nurse?

MARY. Fit? (*Laughs.*) Och mistress you wouldna set your bairns tae suck on me. They'll get naething frae these dugs but their ain spit.

HARRIET. You're not the wet nurse.

MARY. I've never even hud a bairn.

HARRIET *closes her eyes briefly.*

HARRIET. I see. Could you then direct me to a nursing mother?

MARY. Och we've nane here the now mistress. Bidie Begg is back though, an she wis feeding till jist afore Easter but her wee girl choked wi' croup and she's greited a' her milk dry by now. We've kie enough though . . . Cows.

HARRIET. Oh they'll spit it out and scream . . . (*Sighs.*) Very well. Thank you.

She starts to put away her writing desk.

MARY. I can still help you. I can help you with your bags. I can mak you a dish of tea. I could hang up your dresses.

HARRIET. A wet nurse is all I require. Thank you.

MARY. Will it be the night?

HARRIET. What?

MARY. The play?

HARRIET. The company will not arrive before dark.

MARY. Aw . . . The morra night then?

HARRIET. There's an audience?

MARY. Oh God aye! There's naebody here seen a play. I tell you mistress jist looking at your bonnet there is mair excitement than I've hud since Christmas. Fit feathers is that?

HARRIET. I don't know.

MARY. They'll be peacock's will they?

HARRIET. No. How many people live here?

MARY. There's aboot thirty o' us mistress wi' the loons in the bothy.

HARRIET. It's not enough.

MARY. Fit?

HARRIET. There will be no play.

MARY. Aye there will! That's fit you're here fir! . . . Is it nae?

HARRIET. Once we have been to the laird. We are artists. We are not a fairground side show. We perform for patrons of gentle blood.

MARY. The laird's deid.

HARRIET. His heirs . . .

MARY. In Edinburgh. There's naebody up the big hoose noo but sheep. There's nae roof on the thing.

HARRIET. My husband told me . . . ! My husband, Mr Lamont believes we have an engagement to entertain the laird of Auchnibeck. This is Auchnibeck?

MARY. Unless there's anither.

HARRIET. And the laird is dead.

MARY. Been deid five years. Choked on a calf's foot. They had tae bury it wi' him. Can I nae pit your dresses awa mistress, I'll be that careful.

Pause.

HARRIET. I doubt there's any need to unpack my bags.

MARY. Oh aye, jist while you're here. Shake a' the creases oot.

She is busying herself rummaging in HARRIET's *bags.*

HARRIET. I can head back and meet them. We could be on the Aberdeen road before midnight . . .

MARY. Aw . . . Aw is it silk? Is it? It's like water. Ice water . . . aw!

She is stroking and hugging HARRIET's *dress.*

HARRIET. What are you . . . ? *Leave* that!

MARY. Aw it's flooer petals . . . it's fur . . . aw.

HARRIET *grabs for it.*

HARRIET. Put it down!

MARY *hits out at her.*

MARY. No! No! No! It's mine, it's mine, it's mine!

HARRIET *gapes at her stunned.* MARY *crouches round her crumpled trophy, practically showing her teeth.*

MARY. If you're nae deein a play I want the silk.

She edges away, dragging the dress after her. HARRIET *watching her go doesn't see* BIDIE *entering behind her.* BIDIE *is enthroned on a handcart, surrounded by bags and bundles. Her brood are pushing her, pretending to be horses, snorting and stamping and neighing. They push her faster.* BIDIE *roars with laughter.*

BIDIE. Mind! You'll tip me oot!

They wheel her to a stop facing the startled HARRIET. BIDIE *lies at her ease amongst the bundles and smiles at the other woman.*

You were wanting a wet nurse mistress?

HARRIET. Who are you?

BIDIE. The wet nurse. Bidie Begg.

HARRIET. I . . . eh . . . do you have milk?

BIDIE. Well I'd nae be much use to you wi'oot it.

HARRIET. No . . . It's twins.

BIDIE. What age?

HARRIET. Three months.

BIDIE. Well far are they then?

HARRIET. I came ahead. I walked ahead to make the arrangements. My . . . carriage will follow.

HARRIET *sways slightly and puts her hand to her brow.*

BIDIE. Mistress you better sit doon.

HARRIET. I've always had a wet nurse before.

BIDIE. Aye well, I can see you're a lady.

HARRIET. I have never *never* had to . . . (*Shakes her head.*) She has my dress!

BIDIE. Fit's that?

HARRIET. The wedding gown! She took it!

BIDIE. Fa? . . . *Who?*

HARRIET. That girl!

BIDIE. Fit girl?

HARRIET. She was *mad!*

BIDIE. Oh Mary. Aye she's mad richt enough. You better sit doon mistress.

HARRIET. I can't . . . I *won't* sit on my bags by the side of the road like a . . . a . . . !

BIDIE. Tinker? Maist of my family wis travelling folk mistress we niver hud leather bags like yon. Here . . .

BIDIE *pulls bags together to make a seat, spreads the shawl from her back over one.*

HARRIET. I'll have her whipped!

BIDIE *gives her a look.*

BIDIE. You'd need tae catch her first. Sit doon.

HARRIET *hesitates, then obeys.* BIDIE *turns to her brood.*

BIDIE. Bread, milk and the makins o' the fire, then you can play a' you need in these braw parks . . .

The children start to run off.

(*Calls after them.*) Ask nice, and mind the beasts and dinna climb on the dykes. (*She turns back to* HARRIET, *beaming.*) Is it nae a braw day tae be takin the air? Smell that wind. You can smell the corn ga'in yella. Dinna fret mistress you wouldna think it tae look at me but I could feed triplets. If I were a coo they'd get a ton o' butter aff me every day.

BIDIE *heaves a huge sigh. She arranges her skirts, sitting beside* HARRIET. *She leans back, collapsing into comfort.*

HARRIET (*stiff*). I'm sorry. For your loss.

BIDIE. Eh?

HARRIET. Your little girl.

BIDIE. Fit aboot her?

HARRIET. I have lost three. Two to the croup. It's a cruel death. Long and cruel.

BIDIE. Well . . . my wee Effie's braw, thank the lord. Aye and auld enough now she's *a*' her teeth in. There'll be some roaring fan she kens she's tae be weaned but it's long past the time I'd the patience tae be chewed ken?

HARRIET. But . . . The girl said your daughter was dead?

BIDIE. Oh did she? Did she though? God I'll skelp the heid aff her!

HARRIET *closes her eyes wearily.*

If you're wanting tae sleep mistress, I can sit by you. You've family here have you?

HARRIET *shakes her head.*

BIDIE. Freends?

HARRIET. We *had* a professional engagement here.

BIDIE. Oh.

HARRIET. I have *never* experienced such discourtesy. A simple request for food and rooms . . . I would have thought any lodging house *here* would have been grateful for *any* custom, not least a company as celebrated as ours.

BIDIE. There's nae lodgings here.

HARRIET. So I eventually understood. Anyway . . . someone is seeing to our accommodation.

BIDIE. Aye. John Begg set me to dee it. Foo much did you gie him?

HARRIET. Sixpence.

BIDIE (*holds them up*). Twa broon coins. Ach weel. The bairns'll nae be lang clearing the hoose there for you. (*She nods towards the farm.*)

HARRIET. I would like a parlour if one can be made available to us. I need a desk to write my correspondence and to study my parts. How many bedrooms will we have?

BIDIE (*hesitates*). It's the shed there mistress, it's all the room there is.

HARRIET *stares at her.*

It'll nae be fit you're used tae eh?

HARRIET. It is a cow shed? They have never had . . . pigs near it?

BIDIE. The bairns have pit the sow in the field there, she'll nae get near you. Mind you, you micht hae been glad o' the warmth, she's a good big beast, an clean. Pigs are like royalty. Fit ither beast gets a hoose tae itsel? (*Sees* HARRIET'*s face.*) They'll likely ask you up tae the big hoose the morra, dinna fret.

HARRIET. I thought . . . it was a ruin?

BIDIE. Halfway there but the roof's still on.

HARRIET. And the laird . . . ?

BIDIE. Halfway tae a ruin as well but he's still upricht in the pew on Sundays. Jist got himsel his second wife so he must hae some strength left in him.

HARRIET. I thought he choked to death on a calf's foot?

BIDIE. Eh? Fit wey would he get it in his mou? Let alane swallow it? Fa telt you that?

HARRIET points. BIDIE looks after MARY and snorts.

Bissum!

HARRIET has closed her eyes and is holding her forehead again. BIDIE looks at her.

You've a pile o' wool on your back for a day like this een. Is the sweat nae running doon your stays? (*No response.*) You should tak them aff, let that breeze intae your oxters. (BIDIE *flaps her hand at her own armpits in demonstration.*)

HARRIET looks at her for a moment then climbs down from her seat and removes herself to look down the road.

You're nae from roon here are ye?

HARRIET does not turn.

Naw. Nae mair am I. But I ken a' the roads. Far are you fae?

HARRIET. I am one of the Barnets of Huddersfield.

BIDIE. Then we're baith strangers here.

One of her children has returned with bread and a pitcher of milk. She drinks from the pitcher then offers it to HARRIET.

Cold and sweet.

HARRIET shakes her head.

BIDIE. Come on lassie, I can hear the drouth in your throat, you're eating hot dust.

HARRIET. Thank you. No.

BIDIE shrugs, takes another giant swig.

HARRIET. I cannot eat when I travel. All the women in my family have been afflicted this way. Our blood is strong but our stomachs are delicate.

BIDIE (*grunts*). You should tak your stays aff then.

In the distance, there is the sound of babies crying. ARCHIE's voice is raised over them in song.

ARCHIE. My lu-u-u-rve is like a red red rose . . .

HARRIET. Seventeen miles, seventeen miles on foot from Lumphanan. We started before dawn.

ARCHIE. My lu-u-u-rve is like a melody . . . (*etc.*)

HARRIET. Mr Lamont has been singing, to raise our spirits. (*The singing draws nearer.*) Mr Lamont's repertoire of music is not large but he has a powerful voice, it can fill the largest hall.

ARCHIE. And I will l-u-u-rve you still my dear
Till all the seas gang dry . . .

ARCHIE *enters pushing a handcart loaded with trunks, props and costumes. Two screaming babies are bundles on it.* MIRIAM *and* HARRY *trail behind the cart, bedraggled and forlorn.* ARCHIE *spreads his arms when he sees* HARRIET, *belting out the last chorus. She pushes past him and grabs the babies, bouncing them vigorously. The screaming stops abruptly.* HARRIET *hands them to* BIDIE *who keeps the movement going. She turns back to* ARCHIE.

Sweetheart.

HARRIET (*dangerous*). My love.

ARCHIE. Dearest.

HARRIET. My lord.

ARCHIE. You're weary.

HARRIET. No, no.

ARCHIE. You're vexed.

HARRIET (*smoothes brow exaggeratedly*). There's not a troubled thought in my head.

ARCHIE (*beams*). There are lodgings?

HARRIET. Indeed.

ARCHIE. How did you find them?

HARRIET. FULL OF SWINE!!!!

ARCHIE *looks round helplessly. All are waiting for his response.*

ARCHIE. Are the pigs still in there?

BIDIE. They've pit them in the field.

HARRIET. Then what cares have I? Troubles? Me?
    MIRIAM!!!

MIRIAM (*jumps*). Mother?

HARRIET. Take your brother and move to the other side of the
    road, to the other side of the field. Stay in sight but be sure
    you cannot hear. I have matters to discuss with your
    stepfather. HARRY! Go with your sister. (*She shoos them
    away then turns to consider* BIDIE.) The infants have no
    comprehension yet, you may feed them.

    BIDIE *settles herself down as if for a performance, shifting
    so she can see* HARRIET *and* ARCHIE *better as she
    prepares to feed the twins.* ARCHIE *watches* HARRIET
    apprehensively, she is following MIRIAM *and* HARRY's
    progress across the field.

ARCHIE. Sweetheart . . .

    HARRIET *raises a hand to check him.*

    Darling . . .

HARRIET. Shhhh!! Further Miriam! Go ON!

    Satisfied the kids are out of earshot HARRIET *turns on*
    ARCHIE. *She advances on him revving herself up for blood.*
    ARCHIE *helplessly indicates the gawping* BIDIE.
    HARRIET *hesitates.*

BIDIE. Aw never mind me mistress, I'll jist feed the bairns.
    I've seen it a' before.

HARRIET. Mr Lamont.

ARCHIE. My love.

HARRIET. This is Auchnibeck.

ARCHIE. Indeed.

HARRIET. It has no public halls.

ARCHIE. Aye but . . .

HARRIET. It has a population of some thirty souls not one of
    whom has thrupence to spend on shoe leather.

ARCHIE. Aye but . . .

HARRIET. Its only accommodation is a pig sty!

ARCHIE (*resigned to his fate now*). Aye.

HARRIET. I am INCANDESCENT, Mr Lamont.

ARCHIE. What do you want?

She wobbles.

ARCHIE. Sweetheart just tell me what you want?

HARRIET (*choked*). It's too much Archie, *this* is too much.

ARCHIE *puts his hands against her stomach.*

ARCHIE. Tell me and it's yours.

HARRIET (*turns away*). Oh God, a carpet under my feet at least, just *once.*

ARCHIE. In the pig sty?

HARRIET. At least a carpet.

ARCHIE. I'll do it.

ARCHIE *exits.*

HARRIET *spins round.*

HARRIET. Archie no! We need food! We need milk for . . . Oh sweet *God* in heaven.

She stares at BIDIE *for a minute.* BIDIE *nods her head at the bread.*

BIDIE. Chew on that mistress. Go on. I've plenty mair.

HARRIET. Thank you. I have told you. It will not do.

BIDIE. It's a braw coach you have there mistress. Much like my ain.

HARRIET (*caught in her lie*). The roads were too rough for the horses. They are lame.

BIDIE. Pity. Else you could've sold them eh?

HARRIET *gives her a cold stare.*

HARRIET. Someone must kill and dress a goose.

BIDIE. A *goose?* Good luck.

HARRIET (*calls*). Miriam . . . Miriam . . . MIRIAM!!!

HARRIET *starts unpacking bags agitatedly, pulling out clothes, she holds up some shabby dresses.*

(*To herself.*) Orphan waif . . . eight brothers and sisters . . . No, common as beetles on these roads . . . (*Another dress.*) A Russian princess?

HARRIET *holds the dress up to* BIDIE. BIDIE *shrugs, bemused.* HARRIET *tosses it aside and grabs another.*

The Marquis of Buccleuch's wronged grandchild! Yes!

MIRIAM *has shambled on.* HARRIET *grabs her.*

Miriam put these on.

MIRIAM. Aw Mother no.

HARRIET *starts tearing* MIRIAM'*s clothes off in spite of her protests.*

HARRIET. The Marquis of Buccleuch's wronged grandchild. You go to the front door, you sit on the porch, you sob. Any house that *has* a porch Miriam and do not let them chase you away this time.

MIRIAM. But they put a dog on me!

Still talking HARRIET *hands her a heavy stick.*

HARRIET. If your tears are silent, not vulgar sobs, they cannot fail to arouse pity and bear witness to your gentle blood. Now . . . Your mother is sitting by the roadside. She has been driven off by the ingratitude of grasping relatives. She cannot beg for food. She is too proud, so her children starve. You do not tell them the full history, you *hint*, we have powerful enemies, you tease them with possibilities . . . (*Affected.*) What has Mama had to lower herself to, she who played the harpsichord and sang only nursery songs for her own beloved chicks . . . then you may sob.

MIRIAM. Aw Mother, I'll be sick.

HARRIET (*to* BIDIE). She is sick before every performance. Well you can cry at least, Miriam . . . *Miriam*!

HARRIET *shakes her,* MIRIAM *starts to sob.*

(*Silently.*) Better. Be off with you.

MIRIAM *stumbles off,* HARRIET *calls after her.*

A goose for preference Miriam, I can only eat white meat in my condition.

BIDIE. You've never anither coming.

HARRIET *just looks at her.* BIDIE *looks at the babies she's feeding, strokes their heads.*

You've braw claes mistress, easy seen you're a lady but you'll never shift the mud aff your hem there.

HARRIET. I have other dresses.

HARRIET *moves to begin cleaning and sweeping the byre.* BIDIE *sings a lullaby to the babies, follows her in.*

BIDIE (*sings*). Oh Johnnie is a bonnie lad,
He wis once a lad o' mine,
I've never had a better lad,
An I've had twenty nine.

And wi' you, and wi' you,
And wi' you Johnnie lad,
I'll dance the buckles off my shoon
Wi' you my Johnnie lad.

Scene Three

The road, same time.

NICK *enters. He stops dead as he hears* BIDIE *singing, staring towards the farm.* BIDIE *stops singing.* NICK *is carrying a carpet, rolled up, he sits down on it and rests his back, still watching the road towards the farm.* ARCHIE *comes in, walking the other way along the road. He sees* NICK, *stops. Smiles.*

ARCHIE. Fine day.

NICK. It is.

ARCHIE. Are you long on the road?

NICK. Long enough.

ARCHIE. Far to go?

NICK. Nae reason to stop yet.

ARCHIE (*holds out his hand*). Archibald Lamont.

NICK *takes his hand.*

You may have heard the name?

NICK *shakes his head.*

(*Offers him a playbill.*) We have played before royalty, songs, tragedies, sword fights with real swords

NICK *grins. He studies the poster a moment longer, then hands it back.* ARCHIE *sits beside him. He looks at the carpet.*

It's unusual.

NICK. From Persia through Egypt. Across the Mediterranean with oil and figs and peacocks. You can smell salt and cinammon on it. It's a gift.

ARCHIE. A handsome present. (*Pause.*) Who is it for?

NICK. That I dinna ken.

ARCHIE. A fine, fine day . . . I have a wife sir.

NICK. Then you may be lucky.

ARCHIE. She is a rare talent. She can play seven instruments.

NICK. Is that richt?

ARCHIE. An accomplished performer. You must witness it, sir. We will perform Perseus and Andromeda. She is chained to a rock with heavy manacles, all in white. Her lament will make you weep. She has a sweet voice.

NICK. Was that her singing?

ARCHIE. No. A servant . . . (NICK *smiles.*) Her own voice is more remarkable. You will not have heard its like. She is an educated woman and a loving mother. We have seven children.

NICK. That's a lot o' mous tae stop wi' bread.

ARCHIE. Aye . . . Her father is related to a baronet.

NICK *grunts.*

ARCHIE. She has . . . refined tastes.

NICK *grunts.*

She wants a carpet.

NICK. Ah.

ARCHIE. It's a gift you say?

NICK. I believe it is.

ARCHIE. But you don't know . . . who for?

NICK. Well . . . maybe it's for your wife.

ARCHIE. Name your price!

NICK. Foo much have you got?

ARCHIE. The appreciation of our audience must surely run to several pounds, several pounds. You'll never have seen a company like ours north of the Forth.

NICK. Foo much have you got *noo*?

ARCHIE. I tell you man, the promise of our talent is as good as money in your pocket.

NICK. No. It's nae.

ARCHIE. What will you take for it?

NICK. Foo long hiv you hid that servant lassie?

ARCHIE. Eh?

NICK. She's a bonny voice, I'll tak her.

ARCHIE. You're never serious!? (NICK *just stares at him.*) Och man! She's only half her ain teeth! She's a wet nurse, for my wife . . . I couldn't . . . she's not really in our employ you know? . . .

NICK. Otherwise you'd sell her me would you? Hell mend you man.

ARCHIE *gapes.* NICK *reaches out and fingers* ARCHIE's *coat.*

Siller buttons . . . Ach but the nights are nae so cauld yet . . . and it's poor cloth.

ARCHIE. It's kept my bones warm on nights that froze the stubble on my chin. Kept my life in my throat when there was no other shelter.

NICK. Then it's valuable enough. (*He nods.*) I'll mak a bargain wi' you maister. I'll gie you the carpet for your coat gin you pit a wee clip of your hair in one pocket and a wee clip of your nail in the ither.

ARCHIE *stares at him, then he laughs.*

ARCHIE. Why?

NICK. That way I'll hae your coat and I'll hae your luck an a'.

ARCHIE. My *luck*? You're welcome to it.

NICK. Aye well, a wee bit luck's better than nane at a'. You'll maybe miss it.

ARCHIE. I'll take my chances.

NICK *grins, takes out a knife.*

NICK. A gambling man eh?

ARCHIE *takes off his coat.* NICK *puts it on then leans in to trim a piece of* ARCHIE's *nail and the hair close to his face. He puts one in each pocket. He stands a minute looking towards the byre again.*

Aye well . . . I'll maybe be back this way.

He nods and exits, whistling BIDIE's *song.*

ARCHIE *spreads out the carpet. He grins.*

ARCHIE. Our luck's changed.

Scene Four

The farm, dusk.

It is getting dark. BIDIE *stands by her cart and whistles up her children.*

BIDIE. Cam hame, cam hame my wee bunnies it's late and I've food for you.

*She whistles again, warbling like a bird. As she calls, the
children run on one by one from different directions. They
scramble over the cart, pulling out branches and coverings,
making a bow tent around the cart.*

Cam hame my wee doos, your nest's here an it's warm for
you. Cam hame my wee spuggies, I'll feed you oot my hand.
It'll nae get dark this hale nicht, nae the hale nicht, but a' the
beasts an worse that walk in the dark are bold in warm air
like this. Blue air and licht tae see them by. Dinna look.
Cam hame, cam hame, we'll mak fire tae keep the shadows
oot an mak a pan o' broth.

*She's piling wood and striking tinder, placing a blackened
pot on the fire.*

Cam hame my wee foxes, the hunting's done, I'll clean your
claws for you. I'll fatten you up.

MARY *creeps up on her fireside. She's wearing the white
dress.* BIDIE *sees her but doesn't pause in her work.*

Foos your aunty keeping Mary?

MARY *shrugs.*

Well awa hame tae her. I've bairns tae feed and babes tae
suckle. Nae thanks tae you. Go on. She'll hae your tea on
the table.

MARY. She says she canna keep me.

BIDIE. I doot she can. There's nae a job can keep you is there?

MARY. The minister says the world was made by God fir man.
No here. Here the earth's a load tae carry and we've been
made to work. An a' roond me the trees get tae dress up in
bonny colours four times a year. Black bone branches, white
blossom brides . . . green maids an reid ladies dancing their
claes awa in the wind. They're laughing at us, bent in the
fields, noses in the mud. Fan I've tae work I like tae chop
wood.

BIDIE. If you could work you'd be oot o' here the morra,
there's nane'll fee you if you dinna smarten up lassie.

MARY. Far will you gang? After the hairst?

BIDIE. Dinna ken. Up by Strathdon mebbe.

MARY. Tak me wi you! Tak me, Bidie!

BIDIE. Naw.

MARY. Fit wey naw?

> BIDIE *starts handing out plates of broth.*

BIDIE. You thieve. You canna live aff these roads gin you thieve. A bad quine like you would hae every door barred agin us afore the frost came.

MARY. I've nae thieved onything. Nae since you skelped me Bidie. Naething.

BIDIE. An fits that you're wearing?

MARY. You're ga'in tae the castle are you?

BIDIE. Gin they've fixed the roof, aye.

MARY. Like a white star on the green hill.

BIDIE. Is that fit I telt you? I was fou.

MARY. Fu' o' sodjers in braw reid coats.

BIDIE. You've nae dane their laundry. They coats are manky as a stirk's arse.

MARY. I need tae see it, Bidie.

BIDIE. Life is brimfu' o' disappointment Mary. Spare yoursel that een.

MARY. I could be your dochter.

BIDIE. Naw. You couldna.

> BIDIE *turns her back, ducking into the bow tent.*

> BIDIE's *children have gathered in a group around her all holding plates and spoons. They all stare at* MARY *then slowly all stick their tongues out. They start to eat their broth, still watching her.* MARY *walks away. She stands under a tree swirling round and round, spreading out the white silk skirts of her stolen dress.* MIRIAM *edges out from behind the tree and stands in front of her.*

MIRIAM. That's my mother's dress.

> MARY *stops, stares at her.*

MARY. Well . . . it'd nae fit you would it? Dumplin. (*She dances again.*)

MIRIAM. Why do you want it? . . . Will you sell it? . . . Did you steal it? Does she know you stole it?

MARY. You ca'in me a thief? Fit's in your belly? Air an thunder. You've a cavern in your guts. Fit hae you been eating up there? Leaves and bark?

MIRIAM (*smiles*). Are you trying to dance?

MARY. Can you dee better?

> MIRIAM *looks at her for a moment then begins to dance.* BIDIE'*s children are watching as she moves past them, she's good, the brood quietly tap their plates in approval.* MIRIAM *stops at once, startled.*

> The dance is bonny but you dance it like a semmet blawin on the line.

MIRIAM. I've got natural grace. It's my one talent. I hate it.

MARY. Teach me that.

> MIRIAM *doesn't respond.*

> I saw you. I saw you greitin' all oer the lassies up the hen house. 'We're starving, we're desperate aw gie us a goose'. Couldna e'en get yoursel a bit o' stale breid wi' a carry on like that.

> She creeps closer to MIRIAM, *rustling and dancing in the silk dress. She pulls four white hens out of her pockets and waves them at* MIRIAM.

> Eence the beastie's necks are wrung they canny clipe on onybody. Do I nae look like a fox to you?

> MARY *snaps her teeth at* MIRIAM. *She pushes and snarls at her.* MIRIAM *protects herself but stands her ground.* BIDIE'*s brood hiss softly, still just watching and eating.* MARY *shows her teeth to them.*

MIRIAM. I'd like one of those birds, please.

MARY. I ken you would.

> She walks round MIRIAM looking her up and down.

Fit age are you?

MIRIAM. Fourteen.

MARY (*snorts*). You're a bairn, a baby. I'm auld enough tae get wed. I've been wed. Mony a time.

HARRIET comes to the door of the shed and looks out.

HARRIET. Miriam?

She sees the chickens and walks forward. MARY grins at her. HARRIET takes the birds, checks their plumpness.

MARY. One year auld an tender as my ain cheeks.

HARRIET holds the birds out to MIRIAM.

HARRIET. Pluck them. Dress them. Roast them with pepper and onions.

MIRIAM. Where? There's no onions I . . .

MARY. I'll dee it. (*She takes the chickens.*)

HARRIET. Very well.

She turns to leave, pulling MIRIAM after her.

You may keep the dress.

They exit.

MARY (*quiet*). An well I ken you'll nae get it aff me. (*Turns on BIDIE's brood.*) An you'll say naething.

BIDIE's brood pause in their eating, studying her.

You hear the trees laughing eh? Whispering. Nae bugger kens fit they're havering aboot eh? They should hud their wheesht.

She leaps up through the branches of the tree and away. BIDIE's brood put their plates down and start to whisper, looking after MARY, rustling and laughing. They mill around, shaking the tree. BIDIE sticks her head out of the tent. She has a bottle in one hand, looks a wee bit the worse for wear.

BIDIE. Did she thieve ony tobacco or was it jist the chickens? Ach she was never ony use. In your beds, I'll dee the fire.

BIDIE's *children duck past her into the tent, she grabs a couple for a kiss. Then she stands outside the tent, throws her head back and takes a long pull from her bottle.*

Offstage NICK *whistles the song* BIDIE *was singing before.* BIDIE *freezes. She looks in the direction of the whistling. It fades into the distance. Frowning,* BIDIE *bends to light a pipe at the fire. She banks it up and sits in the dark.*

Scene Five

The road, night.

On the road MARY *is dancing and laughing to the same song,* NICK *sits in the shadows, watching her.* NICK *joins in the tune, his voice harsh.* MARY *stops, startled.*

NICK. Do you like my coat, lassie?

    NICK *steps out into the light turning round. Showing off the coat, the silver buttons.*

MARY. It's braw.

NICK. It's a present.

MARY. Fa is it for?

NICK. That I dinna ken.

MARY. Fa are you?

    NICK *smiles,* BIDIE's *song has faded and stopped.*

NICK. Has she nae a bonny voice?

MARY. You're nae my faither are you?

    Pause.

NICK. No. Fit wey did you think I was?

MARY. Someone must be. I was found unner a hedge, a magpie laid me in a nest wi' a siller bracelet. (*Waits for a reaction,* NICK *lights his pipe.*) I wasna a bairn, I was a cat, I clawed my mither and they hid tae cut her open tae let me oot an I cams oot a' blood an caterwauling, 'I'm here! I'm here!'

Pause.

My father wis a dyker. He made a' the walls roond here. But he left fan they'd cleared a' the fields o' stanes. My mither wis the teacher. She taught a' the folk here. She's stane noo, that big een. (*Points.*) See her watching me. He built her intae the dyke.

NICK *doesn't appear to be listening.*

MARY. I wis three days getting born so they had tae cut my mammy right open. Do you think she kent fit they were deein?

NICK. Fit kind o' question's that tae ask a man you've jist met on the road? (*Pause.*) I should think it'd be the sort o' thing you might notice . . . if you were awake at a'.

MARY. Aye . . . Well . . . It kilt her.

NICK. It would. Ken fit I think is strange? That women can mak wee boys in their bellies as well as wee girls. Do you nae think that's strange? It's aye seemed tae me that faithers should plant their bones in a ploughed field and grow wee boys like wheat. Would that nae mak mair sense?

MARY. God.

NICK. Fit?

MARY. You're worse than me.

NICK. I aye fancied a wee girl though. Aboot that height. (*Puts out his hand at waist height.*) Jist right tae tie ribbons in her hair. (*Mimes doing it.*)

MARY. Have you got bairns?

NICK. Nae so as you'd notice. I'm aye on the move you see. Its fan you see four seasons through in een place, that's fan you get the fancy tae grow things. Your laird there now, he's efter growing apple trees.

MARY. I ken. They're nae worth thieving. Soor as vinegar.

NICK. He's got himsel a new wife. You seen her?

MARY. She's naething special.

NICK. Naw, she's bonny. I dinna think he's shagging her though.

MARY *giggles. He just looks at her.*

MARY. Fit wey?

NICK. She's been thinking of naething else.

MARY. Foo dee you ken that?

NICK. Well . . . If you're doon on your knees in your ain drawing room, rosewood chairs and big china pots, and you're sweeping your new carpet, soft as grass and bright as flooers . . . and you look up . . . and there's a man standing in your garden, watching you . . . And if you get up . . . if you open the door . . . if you pull him in tae you and wrap your arms roond his neck . . . If you can dee that and never e'en ask a man's name afore you've tasted his mou you must've been thinking aboot naething else for an awfy long time. That's all.

MARY. You never.

NICK. She said she loved me. That's a' she said. 'I love you', (*Snorts.*) Think she meant it?

MARY. Aye. Aye I should think she would.

NICK. Fit wey could she? I jist shagged her on the drawing room carpet.

MARY. Fit did you say?

NICK. I says 'Well then mistress I could use something for my trouble.' She starts greitin and runs oot the room. She'll've been reading too mony novels eh?

MARY. Fit did you dee?

NICK. I took the carpet.

NICK *taps his pipe out.*

That wis Bidie Begg singing eh?

MARY. Aye. You ken Bidie?

NICK. Gie her a message frae me will you? Tell her you were talking tae a man wi' green eyes. A travelling man. Tell her . . . (*He leans close and whispers in* MARY's *ear.*)

MARY *stares at him, half frightened. He winks and exits, whistling.*

Scene Six

The farmyard.

ARCHIE *comes out of the shadows carrying the carpet. He spreads it carefully on the grass. He kneels on it, holding out his arms to the dark. Slowly* HARRIET *walks on to the carpet. He kneels at her feet. He starts to take off her shoes.*

HARRIET. My feet are all muck, Archie.

He smiles, moving on to her stockings.

Archie . . . there are people near . . .

ARCHIE. Then we'll be quiet (*Chuckles.*) Your pleasure just . . . that's quieter eh? You can stay quiet can't you? This'll do me fine.

HARRIET. Archie . . .

ARCHIE. I love the shape of you, do you know that? Look at your legs, legs that can tramp thirty miles and still dance at the end of it, arms that can lift a cart oer a hedge and hold a man till his breath stopped . . . that's how you hold a man isn't it? When he's in you, like you'd never leave off hugging him . . . and have I not the strength to match you lassie?

He has his hand up her skirt, HARRIET *makes a few half hearted attempts to push him away but starts to go with it.*

You're a tiger . . . a bear . . . the last wild wolf in the western world . . . and I'm the showman that carries you round and shows you off to the world . . . You could tear out my guts and make a grill out of them but I never even need to put a chain on you . . . I'm no afraid of you am I? No afraid at all . . . Half the world is feart to look you in the eye and the other half wants to shoot you as an affront to public decency and private peace of mind . . . but I'm no feart . . . I love the way you smile when I stroke you.

HARRIET *grabs onto him. They hold each other for a moment then she kisses him.*

See? Quiet as anything. You'd have to travel a long way to find another man like me, wouldn't you though?

HARRIET *tries to touch him but he stops her.*

Naw. That was fine lassie, I'm no wanting more.

ARCHIE *sighs happily, leaning back.* HARRIET *sits beside him, still tense.*

It's clean air.

HARRIET. It's cold.

ARCHIE. A summer night with dew in it.

HARRIET. It'll go to your chest.

ARCHIE *sighs.*

The plum tree in my father's garden will be bent down with fruit. I don't think they can grow plums in this frozen earth, do you?

ARCHIE *starts to hum.*

Turnips. Charlotte has written to me. The letter followed us from Udny.

ARCHIE. What about Fitzjohn. Was there word from Fitzjohn?

HARRIET. I don't want to join Fitzjohn's company, Archie. We have our own company. He would make you perform tragedy.

ARCHIE. I like performing tragedy.

HARRIET. It destroys your voice when you sob like that . . . it makes your face red. (*Snorts.*) Death bed scenes.

ARCHIE. What did your sister say?

HARRIET. She's complaining of our daughters' wild habits.

ARCHIE. They're sweet girls.

HARRIET. They did not benefit from my talent. We agreed on that, but they had good figures and some ear for music.

ARCHIE. Tableaux, they could do tableaux.

HARRIET (*considers*). Ye . . . es . . . Caroline couldn't smile. Her teeth would startle the first two rows.

ARCHIE. Caroline?

HARRIET. Caroline has teeth like gate posts.

ARCHIE. Catherine had the teeth.

HARRIET. Yes. Yes you're right. I thought it was Caroline.

ARCHIE. They're all sweet girls. Why is your sister complaining?

HARRIET. Amelia killed her cat.

ARCHIE. Then she must have been provoked. The cat should've taken better care of its nine lives.

HARRIET. So I'll tell her. Also she wants money.

ARCHIE. For what?

HARRIET. Food and clothes.

ARCHIE *pulls a face.*

I will not cheapen the bonds of affection by haggling my daughters' worth.

ARCHIE. If she had children of her own . . .

HARRIET. I bear the pain and she has the reward. My own children.

ARCHIE. Caroline at least should marry well.

HARRIET. Is she that age? Already?

ARCHIE (*uncertain*). Sixteen?

HARRIET. Fifteen. She turned ten the winter we spent in Thurso. She was Cobweb, remember, the dress was too small. We had a benefit and the snow lay up to the windowsills. The house was very poor.

ARCHIE. That was the winter the girl died.

HARRIET. No . . . The boy died that winter.

ARCHIE. I remember. The ground frozen. We couldn't scrape a hole in the churchyard. That wee white bundle vanished into the snow as we dug.

HARRIET. He had a coffin, Archie. They have all had coffins.

ARCHIE. Sometimes I still think I see them . . . Walking behind the cart . . . They wear white dresses.

HARRIET. Well . . . That is how I would expect you to imagine them.

HARRIET *strokes her stomach and says nothing for a minute.*

HARRIET. I've promised to send her half of all I own.

ARCHIE. Nothing at all. Wrap this air up and send it on a coach. It's golden air.

HARRIET. We have the Shakespeare. We still have the costumes. And the melodrama . . . the four of us could do the melodrama, Harry could wear boots and play the captain of the watch.

ARCHIE. Miriam can't hold a part. The minute a light hits her face, the words are out of her head, like clapping your hands at sparrows, gone . . . We should have kept Amelia!

HARRIET. Miriam was prettier.

ARCHIE. Not since she stretched.

HARRIET. But she has natural grace. It's her one talent.

ARCHIE. We should have kept our company.

HARRIET. They were useless. Potatoes in wigs.

ARCHIE. We should have paid them.

HARRIET. To leave us in Montrose. How could we pay them in Montrose?

ARCHIE. Nothing to eat but herring.

HARRIET. Nothing to fill the hall but more dead fish too dour to flap their fins together. At least here there's meat. (*She looks at him inquiringly.*) Well?

He raises his eyebrows.

Have you more business here or will you call on the laird at last?

ARCHIE *sighs, stretching at his ease.*

ARCHIE. Och . . . it's a terrible time of day for introductions.

HARRIET. You've been introduced. He had your letter! He's expecting you. Archie there is no sense in this. Why must we wait? If you go now we might get under his roof tonight!

ARCHIE. A letter would be a better. You're right.

HARRIET. You've already written a letter!

ARCHIE *says nothing.* HARRIET *stares at him.*

HARRIET. You wrote no letter. We have no engagement.

Pause.

ARCHIE. Today, no but tomorrow . . . ? And Harriet, look. We are warm and dry with nothing to pay for it. We can rest here . . . It will be just a few months. Fitzjohn will write. He has only young girls in his company, he'll need someone of your . . . stature. We'll rest here till he sends for us.

HARRIET. No . . . never . . . never . . . *never.*

ARCHIE. Well how do you think you're going to live till spring then?

HARRIET. I'll not sleep in straw!

ARCHIE. But we'll need to.

HARRIET turns away. After a moment, she bows her head onto her knees. ARCHIE sighs in exasperation.

Harriet . . .

She doesn't move.

(*Sighs deeply.*) Very well my love. I'll chap his door and juggle for him.

He leaves.

There's a flash in the dark, BIDIE lights her pipe. HARRIET turns at the noise. BIDIE winks at her, putting more fuel on the fire.

BIDIE. You've a bonny man there. Clever hands and a clever mou. You should keep that een lassie, they're rare as oranges roond here . . . 'Course, fan you've had yoursel a man like that you jist ken you're gantin for anither straight efter an that never happens this side o' heaven. It's a terrible thing hunger.

With one hand BIDIE has a baby clamped on her breast. HARRIET marches over to her.

HARRIET. Give me that baby.

BIDIE. I just got her started.

HARRIET. Give her to me!

BIDIE. Shhhh. You'll wake them a'. (*She looks at* HARRIET *shrewdly.*) You've aye fed them yoursel have you? But this time you're dry.

HARRIET *stops, caught in another lie.*

(*Soothes the baby.*) Paps nae workin? Dinna fret, mistress. It doesna have to be your age ken? I wis dry the bairn afore last. He cam too early, wee scrap . . . Ken that wee and weak you're feart tae love them. Spent half my time giein him coo's milk aff a hanky and the ither half telling my heart he'd nae been born at a'. I still canna mind his name half the time. But wi' Effie, breests like boulders an enough in them tae mak the Don rin white. As long as I get my food your bairns'll get theirs. I'll hae a bit o' that chicken fan you get it though . . . Have you money at all?

HARRIET. You'll get paid.

BIDIE. You can hae my milk fir free mistress, I like the suck o' a bairn. There's a wee bit o' me in her noo, your bonny daughter. You must've thought these twa'd be your last eh? Fit age are you?

HARRIET. You are impertinent.

BIDIE (*laughs*). And you're forty if you're ony age at a'.

HARRIET. I am thirty-four!

BIDIE. Awa! Oh I'm nae saying you couldna pass for it. You've a bonny colour and you've kept your shape but I can aye tell. It's in foo your skin hings on your bones, I can date you tae a month. I can dee it wi' coos as weel, jist look at foo their hips are hinging.

HARRIET *turns her back.*

Now your man . . . Your man's nae mair than thirty-five. Am I right?

HARRIET *doesn't move or turn.*

BIDIE. Aye, I thocht I wis.

HARRIET *turns on her, glaring.* BIDIE *checks her with a look.*

(*Quiet.*) There's nae anither woman in this hale toun has milk tae spare at a'.

HARRIET *stares as* BIDIE *soothes the baby, settling her more firmly at her breast. Suddenly she starts to laugh. she doubles over giggling.*

HARRIET. The pig sty! He promised me linen sheets. The sow keeps trying to get back in! Miriam and I were trying to bar the door against her. She got one trotter in and her slimy snout followed, pushing and squealing and I just caught the look in her eye . . . (*More giggles.*) . . . and I thought now that is how I must have looked to the landlady at Drumlithie! (*Heavy cod accent.*) 'We'll hae nae tinks here!' 'My good lady we have entertained royalty, oink oink!'

BIDIE *joins in her laughter.*

Oh God. I can fall no further . . . How soon can you leave?

BIDIE. Are you nae stopping here?

HARRIET (*meaning it*). I would rather die.

BIDIE. Aw well . . . I need tae stay, there's the hairst tae get in, then I'm awa tae Corgarff for the winter. Back here aboot . . . March mebbe, seedtime. I'll follow the spring doon fae the hills.

HARRIET. Then we will return in spring for the children.

BIDIE. Noo that I would need paying for . . . In advance.

Pause.

HARRIET. Then they'll learn to drink cow's milk. Tomorrow.

BIDIE. An far will you be getting that, pet? Have you made friends wi' a coo?

HARRIET *is silenced.* MARY *drops out of the tree, hanging upside down in the branches.*

MARY. I'll get you a pitcher o' milk mistress.

BIDIE. You've thieved enough, lassie.

MARY. Tak me wi' you. I've a siller bracelet . . . look . . . I've ither jewels as weel. I'll gie you half gin you teach me.

BIDIE. Teach you fit? Foo tae keep your wits atween your ears?

MARY. Teach me tae dance. Teach me tae dee fit you dee. Tak me wi you!

BIDIE. An fit use are you tae her?

MARY. Mair use'n you! Mair use than greitin faced puddin bum o' a dochter she's got! Mair use than that man o' hers that's good for naethin but a shag!

HARRIET grabs MARY and hits her as hard as she can. She hits her again and wrestles to get the bracelet off her wrist.

MARY. No!

BIDIE. We'll hae nane o' that!

HARRIET holds the bracelet up, examining it.

MARY. Gies it!

HARRIET bites it.

HARRIET (*surprised*). It's good metal.

BIDIE. Oh are you nae jist like me efter a'. That's a tinker's trick is it nae?

HARRIET. Payment for the gown.

MARY. Awa! You gied it me! You *gied* it me!

HARRIET just grins. MARY launches herself at her, wrestling for the bracelet. HARRIET grabs a stick and whacks her as hard as she can, hurting her.

BIDIE (*trying to get up*). Leave her!

The baby BIDIE is holding starts to cry. MARY is on the floor, clutching herself.

Aye . . . easy seen fit wey you've been living.

HARRIET just looks at her, patting her hair into place. She examines the bracelet.

It wis her mither's.

HARRIET. And the gown was mine. (*Holds the bracelet out to BIDIE.*) Here. For the milk and for your company.

BIDIE. I'm nae takin her jewels.

HARRIET. I have five mouths to feed!

BIDIE. Well I'll feed twa o' them for noo! Gie her the jewel.

MIRIAM *is standing at the door of the shed looking out.*

MIRIAM. Mother . . . ?

HARRIET. What?

MIRIAM. Harry's chest is bad. He can't sleep.

HARRIET. Two drops on his handkerchief, you *know* that
Miriam.

MIRIAM. I can't find the bottle.

HARRIET *clicks her tongue in irritation. She hesitates, then
tosses the bracelet to* MARY *who is still sniffling, rubbing
her bruises.* HARRIET *starts to rummage in her bags,
looking for the medicine.* MIRIAM *waits, watching.* BIDIE
*finishes feeding and gently lays the baby down before she
goes to comfort* MARY.

BIDIE. Shhh now.

MARY. She brak my airm!

BIDIE (*moving it*). Naw you'll mend fine pet, naethin but
bruises.

MARY. How'll she nae show us a play, Bidie? Fit wey has she
cam here if she'll nae show me a play?

BIDIE. I can gie you a play pet, better than ony rags o' velvet
and candlelight. I'll gie you pictures o' your ain, in your ain
heid.

MARY (*nestling into her*). Tell us.

BIDIE. There wis a fermer opened an apple and foond a wee
man . . .

MARY. Naw, tell aboot her. (*Points.*)

BIDIE. The Maiden . . . aye . . .

MARY. The Maiden Stane.

BIDIE. Aye well . . . It wis the deil did it. It was the deil richt
enough, Auld Nick himsel. She could've telt by the look o'
him if she'd hid the sense tae think fit she was aboot, but he
cams in her kitchen, dark hair, strong hands, he'd a good
smell tae him, like a beast warm in the barn, that's a smell

you'd trust wi' your heart fan all your ither senses are jist
befuddled wi' the look o' him, aw he was braw, an her
makin bannocks, her hands stopped, up tae her wrists in
the dough, wearing it like fetters, she stops still an gawps
at him . . . aw but he was braw . . .

'You're busy there mistress,' he says. 'Mistress naething,'
she says, 'I'm nae wed yet.' Though she's promised is she?
Promised tae the plooman but nae a word o' that fan she
sees his broon een. An he smiles. 'Bannocks is it? I'd fair
like a taste fan you're done, lassie, a taste o' your cakes.'

An she tosses her heid an her hands are suddenly working
fast and fast like she's nae e'en the time tae look at him.
'Ye'll need tae be quick,' she says, 'They're near done and
a' spoken for, there's hungry mous all oer the toun waiting
on my cakes.' 'I'll hae them a',' he says. 'You'll nae,' she
says. 'I'll wager you,' he says. 'I'll build a road tae the tap
o' Bennachie afore you're finished bakin and I'll hae a' your
cakes, lassie, every one.' So she laughs. Her face is reid as
her fire and she's pleased tae be flirting wi' such a braw
loon. Fan she turns roon fae the oven he's awa. Fan she
turns roond fae the sink she sees Bennachie oot the window.
There's braw stane track fae the foot tae the tap. A road that
could tak four horses abreest tae the tap o' the world. Aye he
wis the deil.

She starts tae run. Her apron's flapping, The flooer's still
white on her airms. She's running and running but he's
coming for her. She can feel his breath on her neck, aw but
the deil has such soft warm breath . . . An she cries oot tae
God an his angels 'Aw save me, aw save me, aw save me!'

God turns her intae stone so the deil willnae hae her. She's
wearing that apron yet.

Pause

MARY. I'd've gan wi' the deil.

BIDIE. Would you though? Aye you would . . . Mebbe though
. . . mebbe she looked ahint her and thocht . . . 'Will I bend?
Will I brak? Or will I be a stane?'

HARRIET *has found the bottle. She shakes some drops on a
handkerchief.*

HARRIET. Daphne and Apollo.

BIDIE. Fit's that?

HARRIET. It is a vulgarisation of the Greek legend. The god Apollo pursues Daphne, her mother Demeter transforms her into a laurel tree.

BIDIE. Naw, it wis a stane, they Greeks must've got that wrang.

HARRIET *smiles. She hands the handkerchief to* MIRIAM. MIRIAM *goes back into the shed.*

That's an auld tale. Ken fit she should've dane? Chased the deil. Turned on her heel and looked him in the e'e an then run at him. He'd have shat himsel. He'd've run intae the sea. There's naethin the deils mair feart o' than a woman.

MARY *starts to giggle. She covers her mouth, watching* BIDIE, *delighting in a private joke.*

BIDIE. Fit?

MARY. Naething. (*She chokes down the laughter.*)

HARRIET *moves to one of her trunks and throws it open. She pulls out a dress and holds it against herself, showing it off to* MARY.

HARRIET. Roxanne . . .

MARY *edges forward, fascinated.*

BIDIE (*warning*). Mary . . .

HARRIET *lets* MARY *finger the dress. She picks up another.*

HARRIET. Lady Macbeth.

BIDIE *pulls a cloth against her for an apron.*

BIDIE. A farmer's wife. Weel respected.

HARRIET (*another gown*). This is for the farce, of course we don't have a large enough company to play it now.

BIDIE (*pulls the cloth over her head*). A feed lassie. Still weel respected, Mary.

HARRIET (*another dress*). Andromeda, it can also be Titania with the cloak, see?

BIDIE (*clasping her hands together*). The minister's wife. He's
nae the breath, the strength or the inclination tae wed
onybody but if he did she'd be *weel* respected.

HARRIET (*stroking the last dress reverentially*). Juliet. I can
still play the part.

BIDIE. An fit ither women will you find in these parts, Mary?
Fit kind o' women walk the roads? A tinker. An actress. A
hoor. Nae respectability at a' unless they've siller tae buy it.
Fars your siller, mistress?

HARRIET (*ignoring* BIDIE). The pain's better isn't it?

MARY. Aye.

HARRIET. Did I tell you about my first husband?

MARY (*bemused*). Naw . . .

HARRIET. Oh . . . You'd have taken him for an officer. His
back was so straight, his eye so clear . . . He was very
handsome. I was seventeen when I saw him first. I was
sitting at the parlour window and I saw him marching down
the street, winding his moustache round his finger till it
curled like a cockerel's tail . . . 'Why Izzie,' I said, Izzie
was my maid, 'Izzie you never told me the regiment had
returned.' I was at that time expectant of a proposal from a
lieutenant with £500 a year at least . . . 'Why ma'am,' says
Izzie watching John stride under our window with a whistle
on his lips. 'That's not an officer, that's one of the players.'
And John looked up. He looked up at me, Mary . . .

MARY. Aye?

HARRIET. He looked at me for five minutes. He stood on the
street and he stared.

The next night I saw him shining in the dark, golden in the
light of a hundred candles, swearing love to the sweating
matrons in the pit but meaning it all for me.

The first time I met him face to face I said, 'Take me with
you, teach me how to do what you do.'

MARY (*spellbound now*). Fit happened?

HARRIET. We eloped.

*MARY gasps. BIDIE laughs. MIRIAM has edged back to
the door of the shed, watching and listening. She starts to
cough.*

Miriam! You will not get a cough, Miriam. Your stepfather
is going to get a cough. I cannot have two coughs in the
family. *Miriam!*

MIRIAM *chokes into silence.*

We eloped at midnight. I took nothing but my mother's
jewels and some of my dresses. I wore them all. Five dresses
one on top of the other. When he put his arms round me he
thought he held a feather mattress. We laughed. It was the
first time any man had touched me, the first kiss I'd ever
known except my father's.

MARY. Aw God! Did you faint?

HARRIET. No, I got behind him on his horse. I held him tight.
I closed my eyes. We left my house, my family, my name,
my fortune, everything. We galloped past the fields and
streams of all my nursery games and I saw nothing but the
dark, felt nothing but his back against my cheek, heard
nothing but the hooves and the wind. I was seventeen when I
first played Juliet, new to my art and new to my love. I
looked down at him, throwing his words out into the smoky
dark for me to catch. He came and called for me under my
father's window and I climbed down to him.

BIDIE *laughs.*

BIDIE. Are you wed at all, mistress?

HARRIET *passes her the baby without comment. She is
performing just for MARY.*

HARRIET. We went north. I was Juliet every night for three
months.

*She pulls out Juliet's dress and holds it against herself to
demonstrate, then she holds it against MARY.*

BIDIE (*to MIRIAM*). Is this your faither?

MIRIAM *nods.*

Is he dead then or did he dump her?

MIRIAM. He's dead.

HARRIET. We were a company of ten, then twenty. The bills of our performances were posted from Leeds to Dundee, my name, in letters five . . . inches . . . high. My father wrote that I was dead to him. It meant *nothing*. They saw *me* shining out of the dark and they *wept* and they *sighed* and they thought they were dead of love.

MARY. Aw help me.

HARRIET. I bore two children at the back of a stage with only the company to help me when they were not required in their parts. Each time, Mary, each time I rose from my child bed, put that new thing in a basket and walked out on stage to say my lines, to *dazzle* them and the *pain* was nothing, the fear and the *blood* were nothing because they saw me and I was transformed.

BIDIE. Noo if that's true mistress you must be awfy lucky wi your labour, but you've the hips fir it, it could be so.

HARRIET. There is nothing, nothing you cannot be when their eyes are on you. *Nothing*.

She is on top of MARY, *staring at her compellingly.* MARY *is spellbound.*

BIDIE. Well . . . you better reckon on being a woman wi' the rent in her pocket if you've a fancy for better lodgings than the pig hoose.

HARRIET *ignores her. She smiles sweetly at* MARY.

HARRIET. Give me the silver. I'll teach you.

MARY. Aw. (*She stretches out her hand, then snatches it back.*) Teach me first.

HARRIET *sucks in her breath in anger.*

I've ither jewels an a'.

BIDIE *shakes her head.*

HARRIET. Very well. Very well I'll teach you.

MARY *laughs. She throws the bracelet at* HARRIET *and runs out into the dark.*

BIDIE. She's nae mither. She's nae even her wits.

HARRIET. She wants to learn.

BIDIE. She doesna ken fit she wants.

HARRIET *holds the bracelet out to* BIDIE.

HARRIET. Here.

BIDIE *gapes at her.*

It was a gift.

BIDIE. I telt you. I dinna want it.

HARRIET (*waves the bracelet*). A roof over your head till the ice thaws.

BIDIE. An fit'll keep the snaw aff your heid?

HARRIET. She has other jewels.

BIDIE. You'll never get the better o' Mary.

HARRIET. She wants to learn.

BIDIE. Well I've got mysel a bed for the winter and naething tae dee for it but wash claes.

HARRIET. Where?

BIDIE. I telt you. Corgarff Castle.

Pause.

HARRIET. A castle!?

BIDIE. It's jist a garrison.

HARRIET. A garrison? There are *soldiers* here?

BIDIE. Well they've reid coats on their backs I dinna ken fit else you could ca' them.

HARRIET. *Officers?*

BIDIE. Mebbe.

HARRIET *stares at her a moment then she laughs.*

HARRIET. Our luck has changed. Miriam! Go and fetch your stepfather! NO! . . . Wait. We should prepare . . . Get me the brown trunk. We'll show him how this will work. It *will* work.

HARRIET *starts to drag out luggage, throwing dresses around again.*

God forgive me. I had lost hope. I had lost it entirely. You
remember what your father said Miriam. There is always
another town. And I was thinking of spending even *one
night* in a pig sty . . .

BIDIE. My cousin Dod saw a play one time, at Aberdeen.
Didna catch a word o' it, he says, but it was naething but
murder efter murder. That wis Shakespeare or fitever they
cry him, he'd penned the thing. Naething but murders.

HARRIET. Why did I give her the wedding dress! Miriam,
look for the white organdie.

BIDIE. Dod says if they could've got on wi' the killing it
wouldna've been sae bad but they were that long talking
aboot it by the time they got roond tae stabbing folk he was
near asleep. Noo Dod went tae fee fan he was fourteen but
he can *read*. Do you see fit I'm saying?

HARRIET. I have played all the Shakesperean heroines.

BIDIE. So you telt us. See these sodjers . . . Well there's half of
them fae *England*, mistress. They've nae education at a'. If
you're desperate tae dee a show mistress, dee it here. They'd
hae pleasure in it.

HARRIET. And what will they pay me?

BIDIE. They're good hearted folk. They've never seen a show.
They'll *feed* you.

HARRIET. And what will they *pay* me? I am not a beggar.

BIDIE. Naw. You're a thief.

MIRIAM. We're not! We're *not*! Don't you say that! Don't
you ever say that!

BIDIE *gapes.* MIRIAM *stands shaking with rage.*
HARRIET *strokes her hair gently.*

HARRIET. Brush your hair down, Miriam. And take your
dress off.

MIRIAM *wilts.*

MIRIAM. No.

HARRIET. When did you last practise?

MIRIAM. We've been walking all day.

HARRIET starts to wrench at MIRIAM's buttons. MIRIAM tears herself free, then slowly starts to take the dress off herself.

HARRIET is hustling MIRIAM into a white organdie dress. MIRIAM pulls it up at the front. HARRIET pulls it down again, studying the effect.

BIDIE. I brak the sergeant's nose last Christmas. My Teenies jist thirteen. Braw yella hair. He caught her by the stream. I caught him a minute later. Teenie near bit his thumb aff. I turned his face tae a meat pudding. Fit are you deein mistress? They're *sodjers*.

HARRIET. Then they'll know beauty when they see it. Men that might have seen death. Mistress Begg, we have entertained regiments many times. We know what we are about. Now dance, Miriam.

MIRIAM shakes her head, nearly crying. HARRIET pulls the dress off her shoulders, shakes out the skirts. She is gentle but inflexible.

Dance.

MIRIAM. There's no music.

HARRIET. There will be music at the castle.

BIDIE. Aye. The corporal plays the moothy. They're only here tae stop the peer folk makin whisky, mistress, they've nae medals . . . or pianos.

HARRIET. Dance.

MIRIAM bows her head, crying now. HARRIET slaps at her.

Miriam!

BIDIE (*to HARRIET*). Aw behave! (*Quiet.*) Listen lassie, listen . . .

Quiet at first. BIDIE starts to sing, mouth music, a dense rhythm of words. MIRIAM raises her head and stares at her. She sniffs, rubbing her face, then she starts to dance. Stumbling at first, she gains confidence as BIDIE's song swells in volume. BIDIE claps her hands encouragingly. HARRIET smiles.

ARCHIE *has wandered slowly on to stand looking at the two women.*

HARRIET. Archie! Archie! There's better luck! There's better luck! Listen . . .

ARCHIE. Miriam, why are you in costume?

HARRIET. A real audience . . . (*She registers his expression.*) What is it?

ARCHIE. We have to leave at once.

HARRIET (*she registers his expression*). What? What's happened?

ARCHIE. There are thieves abroad, travelling rogues. One of them stole the drawing room carpet from the laird's house.

HARRIET *gasps.*

Another stole four chickens from his hen house.

HARRIET. But didn't you tell him . . . Archie didn't you explain to him how? . . .

ARCHIE. I thought it better not to speak to him. The carpet we can abandon of course. I know nothing of chickens, we have not eaten. He cannot accuse us. If we go now . . .

Pause.

I would have spoken with him, Harriet but . . . My linen is dirty. (*He pats his necktie.*) Do you see? I can't convince myself we seem above suspicion. (*He gazes at her helplessly.*)

HARRIET. Well . . . It's as well I have secured us another engagement. We will entertain the garrison at Corgarff, Archie. Military men will have the broadness of experience to appreciate our talents. Pack the bags.

ARCHIE. *What?*

HARRIET. We'll leave! Get the bags.

ARCHIE *looks round him, bemused.*

BIDIE. Dinna look at me maister, I'm stopping here.

The babies are screaming again. HARRIET *is grabbing clothes, forcing them into her trunk, anyhow.*

HARRIET. Young beauty is exactly what the soldiers will be starved for. Look. Do you see?

ARCHIE. What?

HARRIET. *Virginal* beauty. *Purity*, Archie . . .

BIDIE. God help you . . .

HARRIET. . . . and comic songs. *Comedy*, Archie, no death bed speeches.

BIDIE. And fit aboot your bairns?

HARRIET. I'll feed them!

BIDIE. Fit wi'?! (*Gentler.*) I'll feed your bairns. I'll keep them. Cam back for them in the spring if you want. They'll nae ken you then.

HARRIET. No!

She grabs at the twins. The two women struggle for possession of the babies. MARY walks in. She stands astonished.

ARCHIE. Harriet!

ARCHIE pulls her off BIDIE. HARRIET stares hatred at her. She holds out her arms for the babies.

HARRIET. Give me my children.

BIDIE passes them over.

BIDIE. You'll starve them.

HARRIET. They are mine to starve.

ARCHIE. Harriet . . .

HARRIET. I know what I am about, Archie! This is Mary, she'll be our pupil. Get your things, Mary, we're leaving at once.

MARY dithers, bemused.

MARY. I should mebbe say cheerio to my aunty. She'll no like me going.

HARRIET. Leave her a note. Tell her you're running away with the players. In my experience families rarely trouble you after that . . . Archie?

He's standing looking at the ground. HARRIET *goes to embrace him.*

A new audience, Archie . . . Another town.

Slowly he grins at her.

ARCHIE. Better luck?

HARRIET. Our luck. Get the bags.

They kiss. ARCHIE *moves into the shed to get the luggage.*

MARY. Bidie?

BIDIE. You're ga'in wi' these gang aboots are you?

MARY. Aye.

BIDIE *snorts.*

I'd a message tae gie you.

BIDIE. Fa fae?

MARY. A man wi' green eyes. A travelling man.

BIDIE *freezes.*

BIDIE. Fit did he say?

MARY. He said tae tell you, the deils nae feart o' onything.

BIDIE *doesn't move for a long moment, staring at* MARY.

BIDIE. Far did he go?

MARY. He wis walking north.

BIDIE *still stands frozen then she turns to* HARRIET.

BIDIE. I'll feed your bairns, mistress. We've tae walk the same road. I'll be at your back. I'll be ahead of you afore noon. *Bairnies!* Stir yoursels!

BIDIE *ducks into the bow tent.* HARRIET *gapes, then laughs in delight.*

HARRIET. Then all is settled! Mary, get your things. Miriam, change into your travelling clothes.

MARY *runs off.* HARRIET *follows* ARCHIE.

MIRIAM *walks over to the dyke and picks up a large loose stone. She looks round. She is alone. She walks forward. She points her toes elegantly, looking down at her bare feet.*

MIRIAM (*whispers*). Natural grace.

She slams the rock down on one foot and doubles up with pain.

Mother . . . Mother . . . I'm lame.

She's crying and laughing together.

I'm *lame*.

Scene Seven

The road, just before dawn.

BIDIE *is pulled on by her brood, enthroned on the hand cart again, the babies in her arms. The brood are wearing the heads of animals, foxes, hares, cats and crows.*

BIDIE. I had a boy once. A man. Aw but he was braw. He was the ither half o' me. Fan he stroked my face I'd greit. It felt like we'd baith cam hame. The deil kilt him.

The deil cam fan he lay atween my legs and crawled intae his hairt and kilt my bonny loon deider than ice. Then he wis the deil. Then I'd tae live wi' him. He sat by my hearth an hated me till it wrinkled the skin on me. He hated me dry. I had tae get awa fae him. He's aye been chasing me . . . I've aye been feart I micht hae loved him efter a'. Fit could be worse? I've aye been feart.

The brood are shifting about, pawing and snarling, tossing their animal heads. BIDIE *rises up.*

Weel noo I'm auld. I'm awfy. You're nae feart maister? You're nae feart? I'm running wi' blood. I'm dripping wi milk. I've a tribe at my back an gin death taks een o' them I'll jist mak anither. I can cheat *death* maister. You've naething at your back *but* death. You're nae feart? I'll mak you run. You'll run from my muck and my sweat, the *smell* o' me will be your terror! Do you hear me? I'm hunting you! I'm hunting you! I'm hunting you!

Blackout.

ACT TWO

Scene One

The gates of Corgarff castle. A small white, tower house protected by a star shaped barmikin. It's nightfall, an angry orange sunset through gathering clouds.

BIDIE sits in her own space and time, smoking her pipe by the light of a fire.

Throughout her story the others limp on, bent over with bundles, pushing the cart. Many of the children have rags wrapped around their feet against the frost. HARRIET reaches the gate first and pounds on it with her fists.

BIDIE. First you should ken that Forbes and Gordon hated each other as only neighbours can. Neighbours baith wi' lands but only een o' them has the kings favour and that wis a matter o' religion, the hatred wis a habit. It wis a thing they kent as weel as that een family had reid hair an the ither black. It wis fit they were. And Lady Forbes wis on her ain at Corgraff fan Edom o' Gordon cam oer the hill frae battle wi' fifty men at his back. All o' them were hungry, looking for bed and food and women tae damage. They'd a' been killing an feart o' their lives so fit wey no? There's naething worse than death, micht as weel be its instrument as its plaything. They cam tae Corgraff wi' a mood like that, panting blood and smoke.

HARRIET (*pounding on the gate*). Let us in! Open up!

BIDIE. First my lady runs tae the roof and tries if they can still hear sense in a douce voice. Her lord wis awa, there wis naebody in the place but mithers and nurses and bairns. They howled at her like dugs, jist the flesh they'd a fancy tae chew on, soft enough tae mak them hard.

HARRIET. Let us in!

BIDIE. Let us in! They howled. Gie us your hoose and your bodies or we'll burn you alive, babies and all. Perhaps she kent then she wis deid already.

ARCHIE has joined HARRIET to batter on the door. The others straggle on to stand behind them, clustering together, shivering with cold.

The fire took, the smoke cam up through the rooms and her bairns are greitin. They say her wee boy is begging her tae let them in, 'The reeks in my eyes mither, I'm feart, I'm feart.' They say she wouldna open the door tae her man's sworn enemy, they said it wis for her honour's sake but did she nae ken they'd likely hurt her worse than the flames and cut her bairnie's throat fitever? That she couldna save her wee yin frae death . . . or frae fear . . . God would she nae sooner be deid already, fits worse than that?

ARCHIE. Hullo!

HARRIET. Open the gate!

BIDIE. Then they tried to lower the bairns oot the walls. They rowed een in sheets and lowered her doon. An Edom o' Gordon spurred his horse and caught that wee white bundle on his spear. There's the lady's dochter deid on his point. The blood falling through her yella hair. The Lady must hae seen. Wis she glad that een o' them had died quick wi' some hope that her mither had saved her afore she kent naething at a'?

HARRIET goes crazy, pounding and shouting. ARCHIE restrains her.

ARCHIE. Harriet. *Harriet!* There's no-one there! There's no-one there!

BIDIE. The rest o' them burnt alive and naething saved them frae the pain o' it. They say Edom wis feart for jist a moment as he rolled that wee girl's body oer and oer wi' his spear and looked at fit he'd dane. Then een o' his men says 'Would you hae it said you were daunted by a dame?' Then he pit mair fire roond the wall.

The children have gathered in a huddle under the wall. They push into each other, curling up for sleep. MIRIAM limps round to join them. ARCHIE sits apart. HARRIET still stands at the gate. Slowly now she raises her fist and bangs again.

Weel her lord cam back fan the fire still burned and Edom o' Gordon still trotted roond it. It must hae been a sicht o' terror, enough tae mak a man shiver at the power o' his ain ill wishing, the sight o' them burning and the sound o' the screams. Forbes caught him still watching that an nae his back and slew the lot o' them. So mony anither bairnie grat for his Daddy and all o' them long deid noo an a'. It wis lang lang ago but that's foo it wis fir the lady o' Corgarff.

HARRIET *knocks again. Fade lights.*

Scene Two

On the road. Near the gates. NICK *is sitting on a box, watching the snow falling. He has a bottle of whiskey in one hand. He looks down the road.*

NICK. First it's some beast, four legs or twa? Canna see, it's bent oer, it canna get through the snow, staggering aboot. (*Takes a swig.*) Then it's a human soul, still wearing skin and bones, still moving. Man or woman? Canna tell. (*Takes a swig.*) Then it's . . . (*Narrows his eyes, peering.*)

ARCHIE *staggers along the road towards him, carrying a few sticks.*

(*Laughs.*) Archibald Lamont. The most reknowned tragic hero of his age, that's richt eh? Foo you deein Archie?

ARCHIE *stares up at him, his breath rough in his throat.*

Fa would've thocht the snaw would come sae early eh? Aw man, you should never hae gied me your coat. You'll dee.

ARCHIE. You stole the carpet.

NICK. I paid dear for that carpet.

ARCHIE. You took it. Give me my coat back.

NICK. I took naething I hadna earned. The woman shouldna hold my flesh sae cheap, tae buy me off wi' love I canna use.

ARCHIE *coughs, doubled over.*

Aw man. I doot your luck's a' gone.

ARCHIE *coughs again, half collapsing.*

Far hae you come fae?

ARCHIE. Corgarff castle.

NICK. A cold welcome there.

ARCHIE. We were told there was a garrison. Soldiers, hordes of red coats with knives in their mouths and guns on their backs, all ready for battle or song.

NICK. Na it took forty troppers tae try and stop whiskey getting made and fifty tae find the roads it travelled by but . . . they never did find the roads. Maist o' them couldna find their arse wi' baith hands so . . . this year they reckoned they'd let them stay doon south. It's cheaper for the government.

Did they leave you warm beds at least?

ARCHIE. They left the gate locked.

NICK *hands* ARCHIE *the whiskey bottle. He gets off the crate he's sitting on and pulls out another, unopened. He gives that to* ARCHIE *as well.*

NICK. Far will you gang then?

ARCHIE. Inverness! There must be an aristocratic audience in Inverness, don't you think?

NICK. I wouldna count on it.

ARCHIE. No! No more would I.

NICK. It's a week's walk or mair and the mountains get higher.

ARCHIE. She made us walk through rivers. She took off her skirts and went ahead of us. *Singing.* She can't swim you know. For what? For *what*? It's the last mistake. She's made the mistake that'll kill us. We could have turned south a year ago but she wouldn't play matrons' parts in towns that had seen her as a young beauty.

Madness and vanity and mistakes and we'll die of it!

NICK. And far were you? Fan a' these mistakes were made?

ARCHIE. Give me my coat.

NICK. I doot we'll need tae mak anither bargain, maister.

ARCHIE. I've nothing left.

NICK. You've aye got something gin you're breathing at a'.

Pause.

I've jist come frae a toun the ither side o' Kildrummy. Every soul in the place is awa tae dee. An awfy sicht. The cows toppled in the fields wi' their udders bursting an naebody tae milk them, the hens picking food aff the kitchen flaer far the farm wife's lying an she canna get up. It's some sickness, stops the breath in your throat. It'll likely kill them a'.

I pit them in their ain beds an kissed a' the lassies, e'en them wi' warts. They'll maybe dee wi' a smile on their cheeks but maybe no. A kiss isnae much use tae you fan death's got his heid on the pillow next tae you.

So . . . You've a bit o' life tae bargain wi' maister. I'll mak a deal wi' you, your coat for the truth and a gamble.

ARCHIE. The truth?

NICK. Aye.

ARCHIE. About what?

NICK. Fitever I fancy asking you. Is it a deal?

ARCHIE *just laughs, then coughs again, he's shivering.*

Fit wey dee you stay wi' her?

ARCHIE. She's my wife.

NICK. No . . . (*Shakes his head.*) No, no, that's nae the answer.

Pause.

ARCHIE. There's no another man'll come near her. They shrivel up. But I made her shiver. I still do.

NICK. Ah.

ARCHIE. Give me my coat. (*He's hugging himself with cold.*)

NICK. So. You get to be a hunter, a lion tamer, a man wi' a cock that can tame monsters. And you never hiv tae mak your ain mistakes . . . Noo that's a bargain she's giein you maister. A better een than me.

ARCHIE. Give me my coat.

NICK. And won't the cauld kill me gin I dee?

ARCHIE *doubles over, coughing.*

Well we made a deal richt enough, so here's the gamble. I kissed a' the lassies, it'll be death's breath I hae in my mou now.

NICK *takes a swig of whiskey.*

Gie me a kiss maister, tender, like you mean it. I'll gie you your coat gin you can kiss death.

ARCHIE. You devil!

NICK *laughs.*

NICK. At least you'll be warm. Do you nae want tae be warm at least fan death cams tae choke you?

NICK *gets up. He walks over to* ARCHIE. ARCHIE *stares up at him, shivering.* NICK *bends over and gives him a long kiss on the mouth. Then he takes off the coat and tenderly wraps it round* ARCHIE.

There. Feel the warmth o' that.

ARCHIE *closes his eyes.* NICK *looks at him a moment longer, then he shoulders his crate. He turns to leave.*

(*Laughs.*) The bargains a man will mak wi' fate. Hell mend you all.

ARCHIE *wraps the coat closer round him. He slumps in the snow drifts. It starts to snow. He lies down.*

Scene Three

The castle gates. BIDIE's *tent has been set up and a rough shelter built around both handcarts,* BIDIE's *and* HARRIET's. *There is a dead fire with some cooking utensils scattered round it.*

HARRIET *and* MARY *enter, dragging a heavy log between them.* HARRIET *is now visibly pregnant, seven months' gone.*

MARY (*struggling*). Wait till I get my breath.

HARRIET. I'll wait for nothing.

She pulls at the log.

MARY. Far do you get the strength?

HARRIET. I'm as strong as I need to be.

MARY. Och let me rest a minute!

MARY collapses in the snow. HARRIET stays standing, looking up the road.

HARRIET. We should be gone from here. We should have left last week. The weather can only get worse.

MARY. Bidie says we're fifty miles from Inverness. I canna see onything up there but blizzard. The mountains must be as big as that storm. We've to cross that to get far we're gan.

HARRIET. Yes.

The two women look at the view in silence for a minute.

They're only hills. The snow is soft. It'll be kind to us.

MARY. The wind willna.

MARY sniffs loudly, wiping her nose on her sleeve.

HARRIET (*gentle but stern*). Mary.

MARY looks at her.

Again, please.

MARY frowns, then realises. She attempts HARRIET's accent.

MARY. The wind will not be kind.

HARRIET. Indeed. I would be glad to reach the softer country below. (*She passes MARY a handkerchief.*)

MARY (*dabbing her nose*). Indeed.

HARRIET stiffens and sways strangely for a moment.

(*Getting up.*) I'll be glad tae get a seat that doesna freeze my bum aff.

HARRIET. *Mary.*

MARY. Aw God . . . I dinna ken fit wey tae . . . (*Change voice.*) I cannot say that different.

HARRIET. Differently.

MARY. Let's get in oot the *snaw*.

HARRIET. In a minute. (*She catches her breath.*)

MARY. Fit is it?

HARRIET *says nothing for a moment, gazing out over the landscape.*

HARRIET. It's so strange. The first child I wanted as a gift to John. I'd bled for it. I couldn't imagine a present that would cost me more . . . but it wasn't really any use to him . . . Then I thought I have a gift to give the child, our children, they would each be unique but with the look of us, our voice, our way of moving . . . they would be extraordinary . . . I don't think they're planning to be extraordinary do you? . . . Then I stopped seeing any sense in it at all. There is no choice in it.

MARY. I could be your daughter.

HARRIET. Well. That'd tweak fate's nose indeed.

MARY *drops a low curtsey, a bow for royalty.*

MARY. Mother.

HARRIET *laughs. She grabs* MARY*'s skirt and blows her own nose with it.*

HARRIET. No I don't think I'm old enough for the part. Not yet.

MARY. Your Miriam's mither!

HARRIET. Well . . . there is no choice in that at all . . . is there? Have you learned that speech, Mary?

MARY. You only gave it me this last nicht.

HARRIET. When she stands on the city walls . . . They drag her husband's body out, trailing his blood in the dust before her . . . You should stamp . . .

MARY. Stamp?

HARRIET (*stamping from foot to foot*). Stamp! She pounds the wall. She shakes her spear . . . Roar her defiance!

MARY *joins in giggling.* HARRIET *stamps and yells ferociously. She sees* MARY's *alarm.*

But not too fierce. You'll frighten the stalls. The anger of women is an ugliness they should never imagine.

HARRIET *stands still a moment.* MARY *moves closer to her.*

MARY. I ken you're deein right.

HARRIET. You love to be looked at, don't you Mary?

MARY. Aye.

HARRIET. That's as it should be and you can make them look can't you?

HARRIET *sways again, stamping from foot to foot.* MARY *laughs at her, puzzled.*

My feet are cold . . . And what will they see when they stare at you, what will you make them see?

MARY *says nothing. She just watches* HARRIET, *hungrily.*

Oh. I'm to tell you am I? Well . . . they may see what I am. What I will give you. But not yet. Not yet. First you hunger and you want and you despair, then maybe you can have it from me . . . if *I* choose. I can *choose.* Do you hear me? It's mine to give. *Mine.*

MARY. Yes.

HARRIET. Yes. That is what John gave me. And he died of damp in a debtors' room . . . I could not believe it of him . . . there's no sense in it, Mary. You must hold it for yourself.

ARCHIE *enters, staggering. He seems about to speak. He coughs rackingly and collapses.*

MARY. He's fainted!

HARRIET. He's been drinking. Get up Archie, your clothes are soaked.

ARCHIE *struggles and subsides.* MARY *moves to help him.* HARRIET *clutches at her.*

In a minute. Let me hold your shoulders, Mary.

MARY *does so.* HARRIET *starts to stamp from foot to foot again.* MARY *giggles, copying her.*

You're good Mary. You will have a great career. You will
go to London . . . Now shout!

Both women yell at the top of their lungs.

MARY (*still laughing*). What are you doing?

HARRIET. I'm having a child. What did you think?

MARY. Now!

HARRIET. In about four hours I should think.

MARY. Here!!!

HARRIET. I do not think it good he should be born into a
snow drift but he will only have his own impatience to
blame.

HARRIET stamps again.

MARY. BIDIE!!

HARRIET. In fact . . . when you play that scene . . . when the
dead body is dragged before you . . . it would be better if
you do not shout. Better if you stand stricken a moment then
bow your head in silent tears. If you stand well downstage
they should be visible. It will be much more sympathetic . . .
(*She breathes hard.*) Go and dig Archie out.

MARY. But it's nae time yet! Fit does it feel like? Will it kill
you?

HARRIET. Don't be stupid.

MARY. BIDIE!

HARRIET. Mary he's not moving . . . Archie get *up*. (*She is
brushing the snow off* ARCHIE, *propping him up*.) Archie I
don't have time for this just now. I'm having the baby,
you'll have to wake up.

ARCHIE *groans*. MIRIAM *limps on, at her back* BIDIE's
*children move in procession, all imitating her hurpling gait.
They too carry wood. They stop, staring.*

MARY. Fars Bidie?

MIRIAM *just stares.*

HARRIET. Miriam!

MIRIAM *doesn't move.*

MARY. I'll get her. (*She runs back along the road shouting.*) Bidie!

HARRIET. Are you drunk or ill, Archie?

ARCHIE (*hoarse*). Both.

He pulls himself to his feet as HARRIET *stamps with another contraction. He staggers over and lets her grip his shoulders. She stamps again.*

That's my lass. You're near done are you?

HARRIET. It's close.

ARCHIE. Aye.

He swigs whiskey as he holds her, coughs rackingly. HARRIET *whacks at him.*

HARRIET. Archie hold *still.*

ARCHIE. What are you making this time?

HARRIET. A boy.

ARCHIE. Now there's a nice wee change for us. Haven't had one for a while. (HARRIET *breathes again.*) Hud on . . . Let me find the place . . .

ARCHIE *reaches down and massages the small of her back.*

Better?

HARRIET. Put some strength into it Archie, come *on.*

He rubs harder. BIDIE *enters at a trot,* MARY *behind her.*

BIDIE. You'll need to come in the tent, mistress. Quick now.

HARRIET *just groans.* BIDIE *drapes the blanket round her.*

You ken fit you're aboot there, maister?

ARCHIE. I'll need tae let her go in a minute.

HARRIET *hits him, lost in her work.*

BIDIE. Hang on a minute then.

ARCHIE. I'll be alright till . . .

HARRIET *yells.*

BIDIE. Fit's that?

HARRIET. The waters.

ARCHIE. That's me done.

He lets HARRIET *go and falls flat on his back,
unconscious.* HARRIET *transfers her grip to* BIDIE. *They
stare down at* ARCHIE.

BIDIE. He's nae seen that afore?

HARRIET. Yes . . .

BIDIE. Then fit? . . .

HARRIET. I think he may be unwell.

BIDIE. I doot he might be awa tae dee.

HARRIET. Well of course he is! Isn't this the moment of my
greatest need! Of course he's dying! What else would he be
about!? There's a warm bed in heaven and I can't pull him
out of *that* to walk another step can I? Archie!

BIDIE. Mistress, fit you're aboot you ken fine, fit he's aboot
you only dee een time.

HARRIET. Yes.

BIDIE. I'll stay with him.

HARRIET. Yes.

HARRIET *moves towards the bow tent. She drops to her
knees at the entrance and sways there for a minute.*
MIRIAM *pulls at* HARRY.

MIRIAM. Come on Harry.

She pulls him after her in a limping run.

BIDIE. Oy! Come here you! Your mammy's needing you.

MIRIAM *doesn't look back.* BIDIE *turns to* MARY. *As she
speaks she's lifting* ARCHIE *off the wet ground, propping
him up in the cart, wrapping him in blankets.*

Get in there with her.

MARY. Will she burst?

BIDIE. Mary, jist dee fit she tells you and stop makin stories
oot o' it. Go *on.* (MARY *follows* HARRIET.) Bairnies . . .

The brood gather round.

Water an wood an fa's the clever yin that can mak a fire on a snow drift wi' wet kindling? There's a kiss and a honey piece for the bairn that's first. Quick noo.

The brood run off.

ARCHIE. Where's the whiskey?

BIDIE *hands it to him. She moves two little bundles on the cart. Nestling them against him.*

BIDIE. There now. Look fit the pair o' you made the last time. Sleeping through the storm and a'thing. That'll keep you warm.

ARCHIE. There's no enough pleasure in this world. Do you ever think that, Bidie?

BIDIE. I'm sure of it.

ARCHIE. And the little you get you pay for. Listen to her now.

BIDIE. She kens fit she's aboot.

ARCHIE. You had a man, Bidie?

BIDIE. Well I didna dig they bairnies up wi' the tatties did I?

ARCHIE. I mean, to keep.

BIDIE. Oh you canna keep people. There's nae a tether that'll dee the job . . . Aye I had a man. A bonny loon.

ARCHIE *is racked with coughing. She strokes his back.*

ARCHIE (*hoarse*). Yes.

BIDIE. Shhhhh now.

ARCHIE. Yes, tell me.

BIDIE. Oh he was the sweetest lover. The best. You could drink it aff his skin. He jist tugged the pleasure oot o' me. Like my haly well wis laughing.

ARCHIE. Your *what*?

BIDIE. You nae heard that een? I like that een.

ARCHIE. Your holy well?

BIDIE. Your wishing well. Is that nae far you mak wishes? I dee.

ARCHIE *laughs and coughs together.*

Och you jist . . . I jist stretched my legs wide an I thocht . . .
Oh aye . . . Oh *aye* . . . This is life.

ARCHIE. But it's not.

BIDIE. Oh I think it likely is. That's the hell o' it.

ARCHIE. What became of him?

BIDIE. He got killed . . . Far did you get the whiskey maister?

ARCHIE. That tink. The thief.

BIDIE. Far is he noo?

ARCHIE. Over the hill.

BIDIE. Close. I doot I'll need tae chase him fan you're
finished, maister. I doot I will.

Pause.

ARCHIE. I'm sair. Every breath is sair.

BIDIE. Shhhhhh now. I'll nae go yet.

ARCHIE. She can say what she likes . . . I was aye good at
tragedy.

BIDIE. Och . . . we a' get a talent fir that eh?

ARCHIE. I'm sair.

He starts to weep and cough together.

BIDIE. Shhhhh. Shhhhh.

She soothes him, Holding him and rocking.

MARY *sticks her head out the tent again.*

MARY. Bidie? . . .

BIDIE *doesn't look round.*

MARY *crawls out of the tent. She peers back in.*

Why don't you shout? A'body shouts dee they?

She looks up at the sky.

They clouds are coming doon tae tap oor heids. 'Look up
now, we've ice tae blaw in your ees.'

HARRIET is illuminated inside the tent, a silhouette. She is crouching on all fours swaying backwards and forwards, on and on, never pausing.

Fan we get to Inverness I'll hae thirty candles tae licht me will I? A hundred, enough tae mak all o' me shine, won't I?

HARRIET sways.

I want them all tae watch. I want them all tae greit. (*Tries HARRIET's voice.*) I want each one of them to cry till their handkerchiefs drip.

HARRIET sways. BIDIE rocks ARCHIE. MARY watches the sky.

Fade lights. Only HARRIET is lit. Three children dressed in white come on. They raise the side of the tent and look in at her, labouring.

CHILDREN. Mother . . . Mother . . .

Darkness.

Silence.

Scene Four

Lights up. Dawn. The brood are all heaped in the cart. A bundle of blankets and clothes piled together, arms and legs and heads sticking out at odd angles. ARCHIE lies unconscious on the other.

MARY walks on slowly from one side of the stage with a bucket. MIRIAM limps on from the other. They stop.

MARY. I sat wi' her. I sat wi' her all nicht. Far were you?

MIRIAM. I'm thirsty.

She moves towards the bucket. MARY moves it away.

MARY. She steamed. Like a beast in a frosty field. A mist rose aff o' her. Far were you?

MIRIAM. You can drink the snow. Look.

She gathers some up into a ball and squeezes it into her mouth.

We walked fifty miles when my foot was still bleeding. She said I should learn a different way to move. Did you see me?

MIRIAM *does her hurpling skip again, then she hurls the ice ball at* MARY. MARY *covers her face.* MIRIAM *hurls some more.* MARY *hits out at her.* BIDIE *comes out the bow tent.*

BIDIE. Stop that!

BIDIE *has a basin in her hands. She moves between them and throws its contents out over the snow. It was full of blood. It spreads between them, staining the snow at their feet with red.* MARY *and* MIRIAM *stare down.*

MIRIAM (*whisper*). Mother?

BIDIE. She had a bad time. The worst she's kent. I doot she never kent the pain could be mair than she'd strength for. It's braken her. She'll need tae gang hame.

Pause.

MARY. We're going on tae Inverness.

BIDIE *points.*

BIDIE. Inverness is up the hill, a' the rest o' the world is doon. Noo, far dee you think you'll be pushing a sick man and a lady wi' a bairn that's near too wee tae suck? That wis a seven month bairn, it shouldna be breathin air yet.

She wipes snow round the bowl, cleaning the rest of the blood out.

MARY (*whispers*). We're gan tae Inverness. We're gan tae walk on a stage, if we hae tae fell the trees tae mak it oorsels. We're gan tae mak a show for them.

MIRIAM *starts to laugh.*

BIDIE. Shhhh now. (*She touches* MIRIAM.)

MIRIAM (*pointing at* ARCHIE). Is he dead?

BIDIE. No . . . I doot he'll last the week though.

Pause.

BIDIE. Noo listen, the pair o' you. There's my road. (*She points up the hill.*) I've a trail tae follow. It's the twa o' you'll need tae get these folk doon tae the warm.

MARY. She's sewed a' the dresses tae fit me. She's learning me the words.

HARRIET *crawls out of the bow tent. She is looking ashen.* BIDIE *snatches the water off* MARY *and bustles over to her.*

BIDIE. Better noo you're clean, eh lassie?

MARY. I'm tae be a princess. I'm tae wear a white goon and dee for love.

BIDIE. Here . . . (*Rearranging blankets.*) Get something soft unner your bum eh?

HARRIET *reaches behind her into the tent and picks up the tiny bundle of her new baby.* BIDIE *helps her settle it at her breast.*

MARY. Mistress . . .

HARRIET *looks at her.*

We're gan on tae Inverness.

HARRIET *just looks at her, expressionless.*

Fan you get your strength back.

BIDIE *walks up to her and smacks the back of her dress, pulling her away from* HARRIET *at the same time.* MARY *struggles to pull away.*

I'll carry you, on my back. I'm strong ken. I am. I used tae push the moon roond the sky, fan I was wee, I did, baith hands unner it and shoving it through the clouds . . .

BIDIE. Leave her, Mary.

MARY. There's a coach waiting for you jist oer the hill. There is. The Earl of Mar sent it for you, tae tak you tae Inverness. He wants me tae sing for him, it's got silk cushions and a'thing. Jist walk a wee bit an you'll see it. Jist walk a wee step mistress . . .

BIDIE. Mary!

HARRIET. You are mad, sweetheart . . .

MARY stops.

And you cannot speak the lines in English. Enough now.
(*She holds up her wrist,* MARY'*s bracelet is on it.*) Take it
back.

Pause. One of the other babies starts to cry. No-one moves.

MIRIAM *looks round them all uncertainly then goes to pick
up the baby.*

MIRIAM. Harry?

HARRY *sticks his head out of the heap of* BIDIE'*s brood.*

We're going back down. I'll help Mother. You push the cart.

BIDIE. Keep moving, dinna let the cold catch up wi' you.

BIDIE *is moving as she speaks, taking the tent down behind*
HARRIET, *stowing bowls and kettles onto her cart.*
MIRIAM *gathers their stuff, awkward with the toddler on
her hip.*

HARRIET. I don't think I can walk.

MIRIAM. You learn a new way to move. It's easy.

She moves to help HARRIET *stand.*

Harry. *Harry!* You'll have to push the cart. Hurry now.

HARRY *raises the handles of* ARCHIE'*s cart and tries to
move it.*

HARRY. It'll run away from me.

MIRIAM. Then we'll get to the bottom all the quicker. Tie
Father onto it.

*She darts to help him. Children are crying. A chaos of bags,
carts and babies.* MARY *hasn't moved.*

BIDIE. Well? Fit wey are you gan lassie 'cause you canna
come wi' me.

MARY *still doesn't stir.*

BIDIE. Ach, stay here and eat snaw then. But if you're here on
your ain efter dark you'll be deid.

HARRIET. Oh God where will we go? Where will we get shelter?

MIRIAM. We can beg for it. Look we've got the clothes on already, no need to pick them out. (*She supports her mother, moving her forward.*) Don't cry yet now, don't cry yet, we'll need our tears. We'll be good beggars.

BIDIE *and the brood start to move uphill,* MIRIAM, HARRIET *and* HARRY *move down. Suddenly* MARY *runs forward. She grabs* HARRIET's *wrist and pulls off her bracelet. She spits at her.*

MIRIAM *and* HARRIET *stop, then* MIRIAM *pulls her mother forward again. They do not look back.*

MARY *is alone. She howls. She stamps. She kicks the snow. She falls onto her hands and knees and cries.*

Fade lights.

Scene Five

The road.

NICK *walks slowly down the path, carrying his heavy box on his shoulders. He pauses a moment, lowering it down, wipes his face. He sits on it and takes out some bread. He bites into it.*

One of the brood creeps on. He/she is wearing a fox mask. He/she is a FOX.

NICK *sees it. He looks at the* FOX. *The* FOX *looks at him.* NICK *breaks some of his bread. Moving very slowly he gets up and moves closer to the animal. It backs off a few steps but doesn't run away.* NICK *lays some bread on the ground and moves carefully backwards. Slowly the* FOX *steps forward and starts to eat the bread. More of the brood are creeping in. They wear the heads of birds and animals. A* HARE *edges out of the bushes.* NICK *throws some crumbs. A* CROW *hesitates near him, waiting to dart in to peck them up.* NICK *breaks the rest of his bread and moves away from it. He goes to lean against a*

*large boulder on the other side of the path. The animals move
in from all sides, they surround him, feeding.* NICK *laughs.*

The boulder he is leaning on uncurls. It is BIDIE. *He is lying
in her lap and she has her hands on his throat.*

BIDIE. Got you.

Scene Six

*Darkness. There's a rustling, roaring wind rushing through a
forest. Moonlight.* HARRIET *is crawling along the ground, her
breath rasping in her throat. She stops, panting, struggles to
pull herself upright. She can only get up to her knees. She
stops, swaying, the wind roars.* HARRIET *gathers a great
breath and roars back in frustration, slapping at the muddy
ground and her ruined sodden dress. She pauses on her hands
and knees.* BIDIE *limps out of the shadows. Her face is raw
and bloody. One eye is tied with sodden rag. They look at each
other.* HARRIET *on her knees,* BIDIE *swaying on her feet.*

BIDIE. Nae sense roaring at the wind, its breath'll never stop.

*There's a single howl, a dog, wolf or human child distant in
the wood. It's joined by others howling and snarling,
moving away. She drops beside* HARRIET.

Fit are you deein oot here?

HARRIET *makes no answer struggling again on her knees.*
BIDIE *laughs.*

Lost in the woods looking for a hole tae shite in! Dae it in a
kettle your pride'll kill you!

HARRIET. I am not an animal!

*The howling again in the woods. They both look after the
noise.*

BIDIE. You're no far on your road, mistress, have you buried
him yet?

HARRIET. We've found nowhere to bury him yet.

HARRIET *gives up trying to get up. She rests on the ground next to* BIDIE. *The howling comes again.*

Where are your children?

BIDIE *doesn't answer for a moment, staring out into the storm.*

BIDIE. Bairns are naething to him, it's only fear that maks his cock hard. Fear o' the dark and looking for a warm place tae hide fae it. That's all that's in his heid. Battering his way backwards fae death. He starts the life but I own it. The bairns are mine. They'll run him doon at last; fear smells strong.

The howling.

(*Shouting into the dark.*) Did you nae think if you sawed a' that life in me it micht grow intae your ain death? I think you kent. You were feart enough. You hated me enough. Weel . . . here's death, laddie! Taste it!

They listen. Nothing.

Aw God, my bairns. What'll become of you? (*She looks at* HARRIET, *she puts her hand to her face.*) I stuck him first but he came back wi' a rock in his hand . . . they saw my blood, they want tae bite the life out of him, he's running now . . . Gin they taste his flesh will they ever be bairns again? My wee yins.

HARRIET *shakes her head, this is just senseless to her.*

HARRIET. Do you know the way? You found us. Do you know the way back?

BIDIE. I doot I can walk it.

HARRIET. Then we're dead. All of us.

BIDIE. Aw mistress . . . We canna be sae far frae a plooed field as that.

HARRIET. Where will it go?

BIDIE. Fit?

HARRIET. All that I am? I could have been . . . What will become of me?

BIDIE. Fit dreams did your granny dream? Do you dream them or are they dust? . . . And dee you care? What's she to you, mistress? An auld woman is jist an auld woman, then she's deid. (BIDIE *closes her eyes.*)

HARRIET. I still . . . have . . . the dresses.

> HARRIET *starts to crawl in the direction of shelter, dragging her muddy skirts behind her.* BIDIE *cannot move to help her. She watches* HARRIET *crawl into the shadows. She looks out into the darkness.*

BIDIE (*touches her eye, whispers*). He gave me true gifts. I ken the world better fir tasting him. You should rest now, love. Are we nae weary at last? (*She slumps down.*)

> I could feel his breath on my neck . . . I wis a cat an he wis a dog, I wis an otter an he wis an eel. I wis a falcon an he wis a hawk. I wis a mountain an he was a storm o' water. There was nae end tae it . . .

> The Queen o' Heaven's run awa fae the deil. Fit'll we dee if he willna catch her noo? I'm awa wi' a' the life he had in him.

> Cam hame bairnies. Let it be done now. Let it be by. I bide alane.

Scene Seven

The road. Just after dawn. NICK *stumbles along the path. He is battered, exhausted. He's rolled on rocks. He has been bitten on his hands and face. He stops, lowering himself to the ground.* NICK *sits, his head in his hands, after a moment he starts to weep.*

MARY *comes down the path and stands looking at him. He looks up and sees her.*

NICK. Get oot o' here!

> *He turns away from her. She moves closer. She holds some bread out to him.*

> Aw God . . .

MARY. There's cheese in it.

NICK (*quiet*). I'm nae hungry. Noo get oot o' here.

She just watches him. He looks at her, then looks away. She waits, staring and staring.

Fit? Fit are you lookin at?

MARY. Are you sair? You were greitin? Are you sair?

NICK (*grins*). Hairt sick.

MARY (*shakes her head and points to her stomach*). It's there.

NICK. Fit?

MARY. Your hairt's here but the pain's there, a hole frae here tae here, (*Stroking her stomach.*) full o' cryin. Sair.

NICK. That's hunger, lassie.

MARY. Well far dee you feel it?

She goes over and opens his jacket. He steps back. She looks up at him for a moment then reaches out to him again, putting her hands on his stomach.

MARY. There. Dae you feel sair noo?

He doesn't answer. She embraces him. He just stands.

NICK. Fa dee you think I am?

MARY. The deil.

NICK. An fit dee you think happens if you shag the deil?

MARY. I think I get fitever I want.

NICK. And suppose the deil is weary?

MARY. You've got a great smell maister.

NICK. Fit are you deein?

MARY. Warming you.

NICK. You dinna ken fit you're deein.

MARY. Oh but I dee.

NICK. The deil's tears. That's fit's got you going is it? Here's the deil an he's greitin. That's fit you want tae cuddle up wi'?

MARY. Aye.

NICK. You'll be sorry.

MARY. Naw. I'll nae.

NICK. Well . . . Hell mend you pet. (*He kisses her.*)

Fade lights. Singing in the darkness. 'The Cruel Mother.'

She sat doon below a thorn,
Fine flowers in the valley,
An there she's kissed her babe newborn,
An the green leaves they grow rarely,

Smile nae sae sweet my bonny babe,
Fine flowers in the valley,
Gin you smile sae sweet ye'll smile me deid,
An the green leaves they grow rarely.

She's taen oot her little penknife,
Fine flowers in the valley,
An twined her sweet babe o' it's life,
An the green leaves they grow rarely.

As she wis ga'in tae the church,
Fine flowers in the valley,
She spied a sweet babe in the porch,
An the green leaves they grow rarely.

Oh sweet babe an thou wert mine,
Fine flowers in the valley,
I'd cled ye in the silks sae fine,
An the green leaves they grow rarely.

Oh mither dear when I was thine,
Fine flowers in the valley,
You didnae prove tae me sae kind . . .
An the green leaves they grow rarely.

Scene Eight

*The farmyard, at Auchnibeck. BIDIE's tent is pitched as
before. It is autumn again, but a grey drizzly day. The fire is
near the entrance to BIDIE's tent. The shed behind now has*

glass in its windows and a smoking chimney. It has been generally smartened up and repaired.

BIDIE *crawls out of the tent. Her hair is standing on end. She peers around blearily. She has aged, another tooth is missing. She has a patch over one eye.*

BIDIE. The fire's oot.

She pokes at it a bit.

I says the fire's oot an it wis you that wis watching it!

A groan answers her from the tent behind.

God, you miss the bairns sometimes dee you.

She starts gathering the wood together.

It's you'll hae the greitin face fan you canna get your pipe lit. Tak it oot your mou lassie it's been deid twa hours. You were snorin smoke there.

HARRIET *follows* BIDIE *out of the tent.*

She has transformed. She is dishevelled with sleep but preserves her dignity. She is wearing her hair loose, she is wearing paste jewellery, she has a bright red dress on, one of the costumes. She looks like an empress with a hangover.

HARRIET. I have always found that a short nap in the afternoon is the most effective sleep I can have. It preserves my energy and freshens the blood.

BIDIE. I've always found that tae. Fars the tinder box?

HARRIET *passes it to her. She starts to comb out her hair.*

Fit een's that? (*Indicating the dress.*)

HARRIET. Lady Macbeth.

BIDIE. It's bonny.

HARRIET. The school mistress is unlikely to allow me over the threshold in these clothes.

BIDIE. Well noo.

HARRIET. Indeed.

BIDIE. Far has she got her airs fae?

HARRIET. Her pedigree is tarnished to say the least.

BIDIE. Dochter tae a gang aboot I hear.

HARRIET. She's likely slept in a ditch in her time.

BIDIE. You canna comb that oot your hair.

> HARRIET *pauses in dressing hers, glaring at* BIDIE.

> Swallowin my shoon again am I? (*She tries to tuck feathers in* HARRIET'*s hair.*) Here, pit a feather in it.

> HARRIET *slaps her hand away and goes on arranging her hair. She leaves it loose.*

> *A baby starts crying.* HARRIET *reaches into the tent behind her and picks up her baby. She cradles it against her shoulder, it's a nine-month-old child. She strokes him gently, rocking and humming to him.*

> Oh that's better. The quiet would kill you eh? It aye means trouble . . . quiet . . . I'm lookin oer my shoulder to see fit they're up tae then I mind they're nae there at a'.

HARRIET. Keep them with you. They don't need schooling.

BIDIE. Oh aye they dee. Need tae let a different wind blaw through their heids. God kens fit they'll come tae itherwise. Micht end up wild. Wee animals wi' rocks in their hands deein a' kinds o' damage.

HARRIET. He's not waking. I swear he's grown another inch. Look at those hands.

> MIRIAM *walks on, making for the door of the house. She is severely and respectably dressed in black, her hair is up. She pauses for a moment looking over at them.*

BIDIE. That's the school oot is it?

> MIRIAM *nods.*

> Aye well, I hope you telt them tae come straight hame. The haars comin in an Effie's nae shoon yet.

MIRIAM. They'll be here soon. They're cleaning the school house.

BIDIE. Aye . . . well . . . that's a long day fir them.

> MIRIAM *goes into the house.* BIDIE *leans over to* HARRIET.

> Fit's she learning them? Dae you ken fit she's up tae?

HARRIET *shrugs.*

Well you learnt her. Fit's she learning them?

HARRIET. Miriam is self taught really. I wouldn't take any credit from her.

MIRIAM *comes out with a broom. She starts sweeping round the shed.*

BIDIE. Well she'd some great notion o' hersel getting that wee job, a bairnie like her, she didna learn that oot a book.

HARRIET. She was born to play the part. You know it when you see it don't you? (*To* MIRIAM.) Where are the twins?

MIRIAM. With the other children.

HARRIET. Where are they?

MIRIAM. I'm looking after them. They're fine . . . The minister has asked me to speak to you.

HARRIET. Is that a reason for conversation?

MIRIAM. You'll not be allowed back in the church.

HARRIET. Indeed? He's pleased with your work, though.

MIRIAM. Yes.

HARRIET. He should be. Fifteen years without education and now the light of wisdom has been rekindled at the back of the potatoe field. It's a miracle really.

MIRIAM. You have to wear suitable clothes.

HARRIET. Suitable.

MIRIAM. Brush your hair. Wear a hat.

HARRIET. A hat.

She crawls back into the tent. She remerges wearing an extravagant concoction of feathers and jewels. She straightens it on her head and smiles at MIRIAM. BIDIE *cackles.* MIRIAM *smiles tightly and turns away.*

MIRIAM. That's elegant, Mother. The shoes spoil it though.

HARRIET *pulls the hem of her dress across her feet and ignores her.* MIRIAM *has a purse at her waist. She jingles and plays with it.*

They're worn through to holes, Mother. You should take care with your feet. Remember how they were cut through on the walk back here. Your foot split like an apple in the oven. Don't you remember? The pain when I had to dig the dirt out of that every night. I'd've thought you'd be careful with your feet. You'll be lame as me.

HARRIET. I could stand outside the church I suppose, I could sing from there. I've a voice that could reach God on the other side of the moon after all.

MIRIAM hesitates then gives her a little money.

MIRIAM. You don't have to come to church.

HARRIET. We worship as a family, Miriam. You have a position to maintain here now. I must support you.

MIRIAM. Then you should wear a different dress.

HARRIET. It's the colour isn't it? It draws the eye when minds should be composed in prayer. You're right. My presence is too large for the building.

MIRIAM. You could rest at home.

HARRIET. I could wear the green!

She darts past MIRIAM into the house. BIDIE snorts with laughter.

BIDIE. Aw she's wicked tae you. She is. Ken fit you should dee? She's your ain mither. There's no beatin it. You canna drag the womb oot o' her and stuff it intae a better place. You need tae look her in the ee. Close your mou an jist think 'I'll outlive you, you auld bat.' It's the only way you will win.

HARRIET comes back. She looks stricken. MIRIAM grins.

HARRIET. Where are my clothes?

The first and the smallest of BIDIE's brood runs in. They are wearing the top half of a velvet costume, cut down so it hangs on them like a jacket.

MIRIAM!

MIRIAM has her hand over her mouth, fighting terror and nervous giggles as she watches her mother. The rest of

*BIDIE's brood skip on. They are reciting their five times'
table. They are wearing pieces of hat and cloak. They are
dragging patchwork quilts, brilliant colours – all the pieces
of* HARRIET's *costumes sewn together.*

MIRIAM. You don't need stage costumes now. We've made
them into quilts. For the poor.

HARRIET *picks up the edge of one of the quilts and looks
at it.*

HARRIET. So . . . I may not go to church in my red dress and I
cannot go in my green.

She starts to take her costume off.

There is nothing else for it.

MIRIAM. You wouldn't *dare!*

HARRIET. At least I have my hat.

She stands in her petticoats grinning at MIRIAM. *She puts
her pipe between her teeth.*

Light me, Bidie.

BIDIE *holds up a spill from the fire and lights the pipe
from it.*

MIRIAM. No.

HARRIET. Then I need new clothes.

MIRIAM. You have clothes. It was only the costumes.

HARRIET. Then I need new costumes.

MIRIAM. What for?

HARRIET *starts to sing a hymn, with growing volume.*

I'll get you clothes!

HARRIET. I could never wear your taste, Miriam. Never. You
have no talent for it. You couldn't dress a chicken.

MIRIAM *hands her some more money.*

I'll have to travel into Aberdeen.

MIRIAM. I'll get no more till Christmas.

HARRIET *just holds out her hand.*

We'll have to live off soup and crusts!

HARRIET. But we'll have quilts to keep us warm.

MIRIAM. No! That's enough! NO!

She runs into the house. HARRIET *bites the coins she's been given.*

BIDIE. Enough tae buy them new?

HARRIET (*stricken, quiet*). No. Of course not. Not one gown.

BIDIE *looks at her for a minute then turns to the brood, cuddling the nearest.*

BIDIE. Fa's that I heard counting? Fa's the cleverest wee flock o' chicks never cam oot o' eggs? Let's gang awa up the hill an get wood an dee that for me again. You're wiser than foxes, the hale crowd o' you. Bring Effie, Masie.

BIDIE *casts a last look back at* HARRIET *who is fingering the quilts, then follows her children off.*

HARRIET (*touching the material*). Roxanne . . . Titania . . . Juliet . . .

The baby starts to cry again. After a moment HARRIET *gathers up the quilt and goes over to it. She wraps it up gently then raises it to feed.*

Straight legs. walking legs. You'll be running faster than me. I won't catch you. You can sit up. You've got hair. Choking with life aren't you? (*Laughs stroking his back.*) Slowly. Why didn't the cold eat you up when you were tiny? It ate your Daddy and he was so-o-o-o much bigger, yes he was. Tell me why you stayed with me, sweet thing? Tell me how?

HARRIET *starts to sing a lullaby again.*

MARY *comes staggering along the road. She is nine months' gone. Her clothes are in rags.* HARRIET *looks up, startled.*

MARY. It's going to kill me. It's the deil's bairn.

Scene Nine

The farmyard. Dawn.

BIDIE *and* HARRIET *walk slowly out of the house.* HARRIET *is carrying the new born baby, wrapped in one of the quilts. They are both bent over it.*

BIDIE. Let's see you noo. Let's see you in mair light . . . Hush now . . . Shoosh . . . You'll nae get fed there pet. Your mammy needs tae rest then you'll get your belly filled . . .

HARRIET. She can smell my milk.

BIDIE. I doot she's the strength tae feed. Wee scrap. Aw wee spuggie. You're nae meant tae be alive are you?

HARRIET. She is alive.

BIDIE. I doot she's jist here for the day. She's nae stopping.

HARRIET. She might.

BIDIE. Well . . . Fit will wee Mary dee then?

HARRIET. The first ones were much easier for me. Much easier.

BIDIE. Aye. Me tae. Green bones.

HARRIET. We had money then. A carriage and two servants.

BIDIE. Mebbe her aunty'll tak pity. I doot the lassie wore her heart doon tae rock lang syne though. Aw God . . . Is she breathing still?

HARRIET. Yes.

BIDIE. Aye . . . I can see the blood ga'in roond. Her skin's that thin. Will I hold her?

HARRIET. It's alright.

BIDIE *hesitates a minute then she pats* HARRIET's *shoulder.*

BIDIE. Dinna stop oot here. The cauld'll kill her for sure. Freeze her lungs and stop that wee bird heart.

HARRIET. Yes.

BIDIE. I doot she'll nae live onyway.

HARRIET. She might.

BIDIE *goes into the house.* HARRIET *rocks the baby for a moment, then she gently lays it on the ground. Slowly she starts to unwrap its coverings. The baby cries. A tiny weak sound.* HARRIET *stops.*

Oh God. I didn't think you had a voice . . . It's just the cold, sweetheart . . . You won't feel it soon . . . It'll be alright . . . It'll be dark and quiet . . . and mother won't worry about you . . . and you won't worry at all . . .

HARRIET *moves away from the baby, staring at it lying, unprotected. She watches it for a long time. She is crying.*

Shhh now . . . Shhhh . . . You look like . . . Oh you look like . . . I don't remember. I don't remember which of them it was but I know she's dead. She died before she ever got skirts past her knees. I remember looking at her watching the sky from the back of the cart I was pushing. She was too little to walk the road. And she said 'Bird', She pointed at a peewit and said . . . 'Bird'.

I remember thinking she could well be dead before the winter had done with us because her chest was thick already. Half of me was too tired to look at her with all the nursing and praying and work she'd be to me only to die in the end anyway.

Pause. HARRIET *moves closer to look at the baby. She reaches out to touch it gently, stroking its head.*

She saw the peewit and she smiled. I smiled as well. She didn't think or care past that moment. She was here and she was happy. We called her . . . Christina.

HARRIET *stops stroking. She bends to see if there is any breath.* MIRIAM *comes out of the house and watches her.* HARRIET *bows her head wiping her face. She covers the baby completely. She looks up. They stare at each other.*

She was born dead, Miriam.

MIRIAM *just stares.*

She was born dead . . . Why do you always creep around after me!

HARRIET *tries to hide her tears. She gathers the baby up and rocks it. She lays it down again.* MIRIAM *just watches.*

Go away, Miriam.

MIRIAM *takes a letter out of her pocket and gives it to*
HARRIET. HARRIET *reads the name.*

It's from Fitzjohn.

MIRIAM. It came in the spring.

HARRIET. Why didn't you give it to me before?

MIRIAM *turns away. She bends to pick up the dead baby.*

Leave her! . . . Why didn't you give it to me before?

MIRIAM *says nothing. After a moment she walks back into*
the house.

HARRIET *looks at the dead baby, the letter in her hand.*

Fade lights.

Singing.

Baloo, loo baby, now baloo my dear,
Now baloo, loo lammie your mammie is here;
What ails my wee lammie? What ails it the nicht?
What ails my wee lammie? Is bairnie no richt?

Now hush a ba baby; now hush a my dear,
Now hush a ba lammie, your minnie is here,
The wild wind is ravin' an Mammie's heart's sair,
The wild wind is ravin' an ye dinna care.

Sing baloo, loo lammie, sing baloo my dear,
Sing baloo, loo lammie, your mammie is near,
My wee bairnie's noo dozin', it's dozin' noo fine,
An oh! may it's wakin be blyther than mine.

Scene Ten

It's a repeat of the first scene. HARRIET *stands at the*
entrance to the farm with a letter in her hands. She is wearing
the same clothes but they are considerably battered. She has

the writing desk out on top of the dyke and a letter in her hands. She is reading from it.

HARRIET. 'My dear Fitzjohn. It is with the pleasure of true friendship rediscovered that I finally received your letter. I can only beg forgiveness for the tardiness in my reply. I realise we must have missed you in Aberdeen and I send this letter by hand in the hope that it may reach you this autumn near Edinburgh . . . '

HARRIET *makes a slight alteration to the letter as* MARY *enters, also dressed for travel.*

'Your compliments to myself and to dear Mr Lamont would seem too effusive for credibility, did I not know to trust in the warmth of your regard and the rigour of your judgement. However I cannot offer you what you request, the immeasurable talents of Mr Lamont are forever lost to us. My darling husband passed into eternal sleep in January of this year. It is only my grief which has prevented me from replying to you sooner' . . . Your hat is squint Mary.

MARY *straightens it.*

'I can however accede to your second request. I was so touched to read how you still wept at the memory of my Juliet, Fitzjohn' . . . That remark he attatched to a request to 'link our fortunes and our finances,' he must be in as bad a case as we were, trying Shakespeare on sheep. You bring no gold Mary and he will be vexed to get no gold . . .

'Indeed I can offer you the talents you so charmingly describe. " the finest flowering of feminine virtues" However . . . I myself . . . have retired from the profession.'

A pause. HARRIET *fiddles with the letter a moment then continues.*

'The bearer of this letter is a good clean girl with a pretty voice. She has had the benefit of my instruction and it is on that basis that I recommend her.'

Do *not* display your legs. He will employ you instantly but you are unlikely to be encouraged to expand your repertoire of *professional* skills . . . which is incidentally a risk nothing but good fortune may protect you from. Eat onions on the road.

HARRIET *holds the letter out to* MARY.

MARY. Is that it?

HARRIET *glances back at it.*

HARRIET. 'I remain your affectionate colleague' etc. etc . . .

MARY. Can you nae say that I'm . . .

HARRIET. MARY!

MARY (*swallows, accent*). I was hoping you would tell him I was extremely . . . talented.

HARRIET. That is for you to prove.

MARY. But I'm . . . I am a bit afraid.

HARRIET. I was sick with terror when I climbed out of my father's window.

MARY. Aye but you had a man.

Pause.

HARRIET. I have come to live in Auchnibeck and terrorise the hen wife. If you make it as far as Maryculter you'll have improved yourself.

MARY *looks at the sky.*

MARY. There's a storm coming.

HARRIET. Don't wait to shelter. Start on your road.

MARY. Will I not get wet?

HARRIET. Yes.

MARY. But he'll gie me a job. This Fitzjohn?

HARRIET. I have no idea.

MARY *hesitates.*

Mary, do you know what you are doing? You are setting out, alone, to walk to Edinburgh with nothing to protect you but a letter and an idea of yourself. If you reach the city with your body in one piece you will have to find a man who doesn't know you, probably doesn't want you and certainly won't welcome you without a full purse of money. You will have to convince him that you can act and talk English, or at least a less obscure form of Scots. If you can't keep at least one dress clean on the journey he will probably never even let you past the door. You have the red velvet?

MARY *nods.*

If you can do all that, he might, he *might*, allow you to mend costumes, scrub floors and learn every part too menial for a programme note. That is what you are doing, Mary.

MARY. Aye. Yes.

HARRIET. Well you'd better start.

MARY. But I'll dee it, will I? I'll get there.

HARRIET. You might.

MARY. Naebody'd ken would they? (*She looks at her stomach.*) It's near gone awa a' thegether. Jist look like I've hid too much dumpling. Naebody'd ken would they?

HARRIET. Not if you never talk about it.

MARY. Jist tell me again.

HARRIET *shakes her head.*

Naw. This is the last time. The last time ever . . . Please.

Pause.

HARRIET. She was very beautiful. She never cried.

MARY. Aye . . . I canna mind it, unless I talk aboot it. I canna mind it at a'. It's like it never happened.

HARRIET. So start on your road.

MARY. Och aye. Here we go then. (*She hefts her bundle.*) See that rain coming? It'll mak the road a river. I'll mak a boat o' my hat and it'll wash me a' the way tae Aberdeen. I'll come in on a wave, singing and shoutin thunder . . . Fit'll you dee?

HARRIET. Write my memoirs.

MARY. My mammy was a stane. I'm a pebble and I'm rollin awa.

MARY *picks up a handful of pebbles and hurls them at the dyke and the farm house.*

Rot you all! I'm awa! I'm awa frae here! (*She grins at* HARRIET.) Cheerio then.

MARY *runs off.*

HARRIET *starts to put away her writing case. The sky is darkening. She looks up as the thunder rumbles in the distance.* MIRIAM *comes to the door of the house.*

MIRIAM. It's going to rain.

HARRIET *moves over to the Maiden Stone. She touches it. She ignores* MIRIAM.

Mother? It'll be cold soon.

HARRIET *strokes the stone, ignoring her.* MIRIAM *goes back into the house. A child appears near* HARRIET. *Wearing white.* HARRIET *stares.*

CHILD. Mother it's so cold.

Another child appears and another. They are whispering together, crying, 'Mother I'm hungry, I'm tired, it's sore, I want, I want, etc.' The sky darkens. The white children move closer. HARRIET *stands against the Maiden Stone. The children are whispering and talking and crying altogether.* HARRIET *looks back at them. She presses herself into the rock. The whispering grows louder.* HARRIET *smiles. She cries out once. She becomes the stone.*

Darkness. The sound of heavy rain.

Scene Eleven

The road, the evening after a storm. BIDIE *is sheltering under the dyke, trying to light her damp tobacco. It's years later: she's showing the mileage. She presses into the shelter of the Maiden Stone, sheltering from the rain. She struggles with her pipe, lights it. She looks behind her, considering the stone.*

BIDIE. Well . . . there's some sense in it. Fit can the deil dae wi' rock? If he tries a thoosand years he may see it sand if that's his fancy but fit wey can he hold that? The rain and wind will tak their time wearing us oot lassie, an' I doot you'll stand fan I lie doon at last. (*Pats the stone.*) A long haul eh? I've nae seen you these past few years but you're near as good as a roof oer my heid the night.

NICK *comes walking up the road, wet and cold. He too has aged.* NICK *stops.*

BIDIE. Aye aye, Nick.

NICK. Aye aye, Bidie.

BIDIE. Fit like?

NICK. Nae so bad. Foos yoursel?

BIDIE. Jist chaffin awa. I thocht you were maybe deid.

NICK. Naw. Jist been tae Edinburgh.

BIDIE (*chuckles*). The deil's been tae Edinburgh! Did onybody notice?

NICK. Fars the family?

BIDIE. Aroond an aboot. They're getting big Nick. They'll all be gone soon.

NICK. Fit'll you dee. Mak anither een?

BIDIE. Naw. That time's past. Time tae let mysel get fat wi' food and nae jist human souls. Time tae sleep in the afternoon and tell mair tales.

NICK. Am I in them?

BIDIE. I pit you in maist o' them.

NICK. See you get me richt then.

BIDIE. I'll dee fit I like chiel.

NICK. Mak me dance tae your tune.

BIDIE. You're a bonny dancer. Foo did you get sae wet?

NICK. Makin for a hoose that wasna there onymair.

BIDIE. It's aye the way is it? There's a wild nicht coming.

NICK *looks at the sky.*

NICK. Aye. So you thocht I was deid.

BIDIE. It's been ten years. But I never saw your soul pass me on the road.

NICK. An you ken fit my soul looks like dee you?

BIDIE. Oh aye.

NICK. Fit's that then?

BIDIE. Like a wee girl. A bonny wee girl. Jist big enough tae tie bows in her hair. (*Mimes doing it.*)

Pause.

NICK (*grins*). Havers.

BIDIE. Mebbe. Have you drink on you?

NICK. Aye.

BIDIE. Come intae the shelter then pet.

NICK. I'll be on my road the morn.

BIDIE. That's aye been the way wi' baith o' us. Come in or this wild nicht may kill us baith.

NICK *goes to sit beside her. They settle back to back.* BIDIE *pulls her shawl round both of them. They pass the bottle between them and look at the sky.*

Fade lights.

End of play.

Glossary

bothy – accommodation for feed workers on the farm, very basic, sleeping and eating room.

claes – clothes

cooshie-doo – dove

deil – devil

dochter – daughter

ganting – desperate for

greit, grat – cry, cried

loon – man, usually young man or boy

mou – mouth

oxters – armpits

quine – woman, usually young woman, girl.

semmet – vest, undershirt.

shoon – shoes

siller – silver

spuggie – sparrow

stirk – bullock

thole – bear, put up with